Peter Lay & Zaiming Wang
彼得-雷 王再鸣

Yellow Over The Mountain
岭上黄

Black Eyes
Publishing UK

Yellow Over The Mountain
by Peter Lay & Zaiming Wang
© Peter Lay & Zaiming Wang, 2018

Published by Black Eyes Publishing UK, 2018
Brockworth, Gloucestershire, England
www.blackeyespublishinguk.co.uk

ISBN: 978-1-9999583-0-5

The authors have asserted their moral right under the Copyright, Designs and Patents Act, 1988, to be identified as the authors of this work.

All Rights reserved. No part of this publication may be reproduced, copied, stored in a retrieval system, or transmitted, in any form or by any means, without the prior written consent of the copyright holder, nor be otherwise circulated in any form of binding or cover other than that in which it is published and without a similar condition being imposed on the subsequent purchaser.

A CIP catalogue record for this title is available from the British Library.

The English and Chinese passages in this book are not necessarily an exact translation of each other. Rather, the words were chosen to convey the essence of the thoughts and feelings in both languages.

Cover design: Jason Conway, cre8urbrand.
www.cre8urbrand.co.uk

All other pictures by Peter Lay & Zaiming Wang.

Nothing is softer or more flexible than water
Yet nothing can resist it.

Lao-Tzu

没有什么比水更柔软更灵活，
但任何东西都无法抵挡它。

老子

Beautiful Three	6
美 之三	7
Sunflower	8
向日葵	9
Beginnings	11
开头	
March 2016	23
2016年3月	
April 2016	49
2016年4月	
May 2016	109
2016年5月	
June 2016	209
2016年6月	
Winter's Caress	256
冬的爱抚	257
Black Butterfly	260
黑蝴蝶	261

Beautiful Three
Peter Lay (November 2008)

What is, is.
What isn't, isn't.
But a thing of beauty
is and it isn't,
when one eye
becomes another.

美 之三
彼得-雷（2008年11月）

有即无
无，但便是美
我眼中有
而你眼中无

Sunflower
Zaiming Wang (November 2006)

More than once
You promised me
To plant the sunflower
In your garden

Sunflower is a kind of flower
The insect well like
Sunflower is a kind of flower
I love
Also, a kind of flower you can't plant
In your garden

But Van Gogh
He found a way
Plant it in his vase
It's not enough
He paint it in
A piece of Canvas
Invaluable canvas

Somebody like that canvas
I like the flower.

向日葵
王再鸣（2006年11月）

不止一次
你答应我
在你的花园
栽种向日葵

向日葵是美丽的
昆虫喜爱的花
向日葵是美丽的
我喜爱的花
同时
也是你花园
无法栽种的花

然而
梵高找到了方法
把它栽在花瓶里
还不止
把它画在画布上
无价的画布

许多人爱那画布
我只爱那花

Beginnings

开头

This is a book about the beginning of an unfinished journey to seek life through art, a journey that began in June 2014 with an exchange of ideas by email. However, apart from here in Beginnings, the words in this book have been mainly taken from text messages and emails between March and June 2016.

ZW.   I believe there is no definite answer for life and art, a harmonious relationship with the universe is the right direction, that is harmony with nature itself, and it is art as well. We can never catch all that exists, but it is there.

PL.   We must try new ideas, to try to enable us to express what we are thinking. We are beginning to get a feel for what works, which is good.

ZW.   I really like to share my view of Lao-tzu and how to think of life and art and nature with you. Every day has some fresh thought and the new life, we are growing up...

PL.   My philosophy is very much 'Now' and individual. I have been collecting my thoughts on this, combined with others. As you know I have been looking into the Tao and how I can bring it into my own philosophy.

ZW.   Beacon with tree under the wind,
   Beacon with the woman wear glasses.

ZW.   It is more difficult to open to you my drawing than the body.

ZW.   I open my copy of Tao every morning, and read the annotation. It helps me very much to understand real life, and also to understand art and paintings.

这是一本关于刚刚开始而尚未完成的旅程的书，是一个通过艺术方法寻找生活方式的旅程。

旅程于2014年6月通过短信和email交换各自想法开始。

除了"开头"部分，整本书的主要内容均来自于两位作者2016年3月至6月间的短信和email。

王：我认为关于生活和艺术并没有一个确切的答案，与宇宙的和谐关系是正确的方向。那是大自然自身的和谐，也是艺术的和谐，我们无法察觉它，而它却在那里。

雷：我们必须尝试新的想法，试图尽可能表达我们的想法，我们已经感到它在起作用，这很好。

王：我很愿意与你分享我的观点，关于老子和如何思考生活艺术与自然。每一天都有新的想法和新生活，我们在成长。

雷：我的人生哲学是"活在当下"和个性化。我一直将自己的想法与他人结合，
如你所知，我在观察道并将其引入我的个人哲学中。

王：风中的灯塔与树
　　灯塔与戴眼镜的女人

王：向你展现我所画的比展现自己的身体更困难。

王：我每天早上打开自己手抄道德经，阅读那些注释，非常有助于理解现实生活和艺术以及绘画。

ZW. I am thinking what we are doing is a kind of performance art too, as we are thinking about life in a different way, taking photos. A white man and a yellow woman from different cultural backgrounds agree about beauty. I try to understand the western religion culture, you are reading Tao.

PL. For beauty to be appreciated and enjoyed it must be seen. By seeking it out and appreciating it you add to its wonder and by your presence, your beauty enhances it.

PL. I think you are right, it is a kind of performance piece, where we are both the actors and viewers, acting our parts and viewing and discussing them from our different cultural backgrounds. These thoughts open up a whole new dimension to what we are doing, and where we are going with this... What next?

ZW. I feel this life is the chance for me; I like to explore the deep meaning of life with my mind and talk to my friend, who is very open minded, turn to the orient, who is a person seriously reading about the Chinese culture and loves Japanese culture as well. I am also learning from him by climbing his mountain.

PL. I like the idea of mountain and beauty, coming together to openly explore our different cultures and history, to probe the meaning of life, which is of course 42.

42: *As in* 'THE HITCHHIKER'S GUIDE TO THE GALAXY' by DOUGLAS ADAMS

王：我在想我们现在做的事情是一种行为艺术。因为我们用不同的方式思考生活，拍照片。两个来自不同文化背景不同肤色对艺术有认同感的人，一个欧洲男子和一个亚洲女子，我正试图理解西方的宗教文化，你在研读道德经。

雷：美必须是能见的，只有能见才能欣赏它。在找寻和欣赏中奇迹发生了，美在被欣赏中成长。

雷：我认为你是对的，这是一个行为片段。我们既是演出者也是观赏者，扮演自己的角色，在不同文化背景下观赏和讨论。这些想法打开了一个全新的维度，我们正在做和下一步将如何做。

王：我觉得生命对我来说是一次机会，我喜欢发现生命的深意，通过我的头脑和与朋友交谈。一个头脑向着东方开放的朋友，认真了解中国文化同时也热爱日本文化的朋友。
我也在向他学习就像在爬一座山。

雷：我喜欢一座山以及美这个想法。大家一起开诚布公探讨不同文化和历史，寻找生命的意义，这当然是42(作为生命的意义，来自道格拉斯亚当斯的"搭便车旅行者指南")。

PL. As an artist, one can never be totally selfish, you have family and responsibilities. You are finding your way in a different country, gaining experience towards realising your goals. And don't forget we are forging a new kind of art, where all your life and experiences are part of the performance, you as the artist, are central to the performance, but of course others will not be aware of the art of total performance, as they only take part in small scenes. It's only you that are in, and can view, the whole thing.

ZW. Yes, life is teaching me all the time, I experience, I am glad, I am sad, I worry, I am happy, and at last I think. I have found I come to the world. Thinking made me have my dream, I want to express what I see, what I think.

PL. Is this a new art or a new philosophy of art? Or both?

ZW. The world is a stage, also is a game, sometimes, I think God made a big joke, he divided the people in the different backgrounds with different languages, culture, experience and showed them different histories, artists are the kind of people to find out this secret. They have a duty to influence socially with love by their art work. It is the soul and in the spirit of the world. The struggle is to fulfil the dream, the dream is for humans to realise the beauty and love in their soul.

ZW. In 2016, I will keep climbing the mountain, the higher I go the more I can see my aim. My secret is there on the peak, what is that, I am thinking...

PL. I like this; I like it a lot....

雷：作为一个艺术家你不能那么自私，因为你有家有责任。你正在另一个国家寻找你的生存方式，积累经验去实现自己的目标。别忘了，我们在打造一种新的艺术形式，你的全部生活与经历都是这行为艺术的一部分，你便是这行为的核心。但是，他人当然意识不到你的整个行为，他们只参与到一些小场景，只有你自己身在其中了解一切。

王：是的，我始终向生活学习，我经历，我高兴，我伤心，我担忧，我快乐，至少我在思考，思考使我有了梦想，我想表达我的所见所思。

雷：这是新的艺术，新的哲学，还是二者兼有？

王：世界是一个舞台，有时也是一场游戏。我想，上帝开了个大玩笑，祂把人类分化为不同的语言文化背景，不同的经历，不同的历史，艺术家就是发现其秘密的人，他们有责任带着爱心通过他们的作品影响社会。这是灵魂与精神的世界，这是一场实现梦想的战争，这梦想让人们认知美与爱。

王：2016年，我继续攀登那座山，攀得越高目标越清晰，我的秘密藏在那山巅，那是什么呢？我在琢磨……

雷：我喜欢这个，非常喜欢。

PL. Life is a journey that teaches us many things and experiences. We feel all the senses, some fleetingly, some deeply. At times we find ourselves in a place that grabs us and stimulates our senses filling us with wonder that we are desperate to express.

PL. As Shakespeare said, 'All the world's a stage, and all the men and women merely players…'. The different lives, backgrounds, cultures and languages offer a rich experience to those who can feel that. Maybe that's what makes an artist, the ability to immerse oneself into the performance with other artists, to taste it, to live it, to take it wherever it goes.

ZW. Passion and Love are two of the biggest emotions.

PL. I believe I have a passion for life, it flows through everything I do and it drives me. Love is very important to me, it defines the feelings I have for those important to me. With passion and love together, maybe anything can be achieved. However it's a heady mix of emotion that can take hold of you…

ZW. I can feel what you said, you are a person full of passion in your life, this is why you always find and see beauty in life, and you create beauty as well.

PL. In our deconstructed post-modernist society, relationship opportunities exist to experience many things; some within your everyday life, some outside and beyond. These opportunities can take on a life of their own in the framework of their time and space outside of, and separate from, normal life. A different performance.

雷：生活是一个旅程，它教会我们许多事和经验，我们感官全方位地体验，有些转瞬即逝，有些铭心刻骨。有时我发现自己被什么抓住并被刺激，在语尽词穷时奇迹充满感官。

雷：如莎士比亚所言，世界是一个大舞台，每个人都是演员。不同的生活，背景，文化，语言给那些敏感的人提供丰富的经验，使艺术家能够沉浸于彼此共同欣赏，体验和理解生命。

王：激情与爱是最重要的情感。

雷：我认为我对生活充满激情，它影响到我做的所有事情，我被激情驱使着。爱对我来说非常重要，它是那些对我有重要意义的事情的基点。带着激情与爱，也许能成就任何事。这令人如此兴奋而沉醉其中。

王：我可以感觉到你所说的。你是一个充满激情的人，这也就是为什么你总能发现和看见生活中的美，你自己也创造美。

雷：解构后现代主义，关系存在于对许多事物的体验中，有些来自于日常生活，有些是生活之外的。它呈现自己的时空框架，游离于日常生活之外，是不同的行为方式。

ZW.   I agree with you that in deconstructed post-modernism, relationship opportunities exist to experience many things. What we are used to is what we are taught to be. Art life also creates new relationships of how people get to each other.

PL.   Our relationship seems to exist sometimes outside of normal space and time, outside of normal conventions and everyday life. For a brief period of time we make our own rules that only exist within the performance between us.

王：我同意，解构后现代主义，关系存在于对许多事物的体验。我们习惯的东西是我们被教化的。艺术生命是创作一种新的关系-人们将如何相处。

雷：我们的关系似乎就存在于日常惯例之外，在短暂一段时间内我们有自己的行为准则，它只在二人的行为中。

March 2016

2016年3月

It is time to pull up the bed covers and wander into dreams.

I hope you will wander long in your dreams till the spring comes, step on the green grass and look at the yellow blossom.

The Yellow Flower is very beautiful; I will hold it close and breathe in its aroma.

In fact, the Flower also has a heart and understands feelings; it will bloom more beautifully under love. Water is the same when you sing to it, it becomes nice and healthy.

Wonderful thoughts, I look forward to seeing the Flower blossom as it is loved. I look forward to you singing to water.

And you will sing to both.

Ok, pull up your covers and start your dream and me too... I will let you know what comes to my dream tomorrow.

Maybe see you in your dream.

That would be lovely; I'll look for you... Are you hiding in my bed?

Hiding in your dream!

I go to sleep now to find you in my dream.

铺床睡觉,去梦里漫步。

我希望你梦里漫步直到春天,走在草丛中看黄蔷薇怒放。

蔷薇很美,我会擎着轻嗅它的芬芳。

其实,花草亦有心能善解人意。在爱的沐浴下,它开得更美丽,水也一样,当你歌唱,它会跳舞。

美妙的想法。我期待着蔷薇花在关爱中开放,期待你唱歌给水听。

你给它们俩唱歌听。

好吧,铺好床开始梦之旅。我也睡觉去。明天我会告诉你我的梦。

也许我们在梦里见着呢。

那多美啊,让我找找你是否藏在床上?

躲在你梦里。

我真要睡觉了去梦里找你。

In my dream...

The Bear and the Flower

One day a Bear was walking on the side of the Mountain when he saw a small Yellow Flower growing in a small piece of earth. Mm, thought the bear and bent to pick the Flower, but just at that moment the Bear had another thought, 'if I pick this Flower it will only last a short time!'

So the Bear didn't pick the small Yellow Flower, instead he came to see it regularly, he showed it to the Gardener, who watered it, and the Bear talked to it of love and nature. Eventually that small Yellow Flower grew and bloomed into one of the most beautiful flowers the Bear had ever seen.

This made the Bear very happy and he hoped the beautiful Yellow Flower would be happy too.

From the story of the Bear and the Yellow Flower, people can understand the beauty of the Flower. He didn't pick it; he cared for it and made it bloom. The Flower can grow year by year in the wild. We learn from our life experience, we grow up all the time. The Bear learnt how to garden the wild, Yellow Flower and the Flower learnt how to be beautiful.

我的梦

熊与蔷薇

一天,一只熊走在山坡上。突然,它看见一朵小黄花长在路边上。嗯,熊想着弯下腰去摘它。刹那间,熊又想如果我把它摘下,它很快就干枯了。

熊没有摘那小花,而是经常来看看她。还像园丁一样给她浇水关爱呵护。后来,那朵小黄花出落得枝繁叶茂,熊从来没见过那么美的花。

这让熊非常快乐,同时它希望那花也快乐。

(这个故事使我们理解花之美,是因为有爱,野地的花可以经年开放。生活教会我们成长,熊学会当个好园丁,花学会美丽的盛开。)

Spring is coming; only thing I need to do is flowering.

You need a Gardener.

Without the Gardener how is the Flower flowering. However, I am a wild Flower, I need sun and rain, England is good for me.

A wild Flower is beautiful… And with love it can fully blossom in this green and pleasant land.

Mountain full of love maybe the climber can go up to the top.

The Mountain is big, solid and dependable, the Gardener is caring and gentle and the Bear is wild and cautious. The Yellow Flower is wild and beautiful, and loved by the Mountain, the Gardener and the Bear.

The Gardener and the Bear, they are so nice and it's never enough to hug them. With the big love of the Mountain, the Yellow Flower is blooming and smiling. I think it is nature, the sun sets and the Gardener and Mountain need to have rest and sleep. As the sun rises the Mountain wakes up with a smile, the Gardener comes to the blooms to say, 'hello.' The new day starts, cheer up!

The blooms are so sweet this morning.

I am proud to be blooms rooted in the sunny Mountain.

The sunny Mountain is very proud and happy to feel the roots of the Yellow Flower and to see her bloom. She is beautiful.

春天来了，唯一能做的就是开花。

你需要一个园丁。

没有园丁蔷薇怎能盛开呢。然而，我是一朵野花，需要阳光和雨露，英格兰很适合我。

野蔷薇很美，在关爱下才能绽放。

在这宜人的绿地上。

大山深厚的爱能让攀登者到达山顶。

大山宏伟坚固可靠，园丁温和有责任心，熊野性但谨慎。野蔷薇在他们守护下美丽盛开。

园丁和熊那样和蔼不知疲倦地守护，蔷薇沉浸在山的大爱中微笑着绽放。日落后山和园丁需要休息和睡觉，日出时山微笑着醒来，园丁来对花说，早上好，新的一天开始了，加油！

花们今早真甜美。

我很自豪扎根于阳光明媚的大山的怀抱。

明阳山也很骄傲很快乐看到野蔷薇根深叶茂。

The Storm
Zaiming Wang (2016)

I died yesterday
And grew the new life
In the same moment
The past is past
Like the storm beat the trunk of a tree
Ravaged the leaves and flowers at night
Meantime the tree was dancing
And singing by the wind
Becoming stronger in the second
When sunrise

暴风雨
王再鸣（2016年）

昨夜一个我逝去
昨夜
一个我诞生

风暴击打树干
摧残花朵与枝叶

树狂舞 在风中高歌

日出之时
与日长啸

You will not always be trapped in the dark... One day the sun will shine for you.

It is the calm after the storm; Gardener comes to fix the mess, the Flower is opening.

I am rooted in the Mountain and bloom.

With the Mountain the Yellow Flower can relax to be beautiful.

From ugly you see beautiful, from ruin you know life; from cruel you understand love...

It is hard when you feel pain. I have known sadness and pain in my life, it is hard to keep going and keep purpose in your life.

When you hate you will not have tears when you feel love you have tears.

The Mountain sees and feels lots of things, it doesn't understand them all, but that is life...

In the deep of my heart I hide the real love, in the surface I hate, I cry, I fight to survive and win.

你不会永远被困在黑暗中,太阳终会照耀你。

风暴之后一片寂静,园叔默默收拾一片狼藉,蔷薇默默地开放。

从丑恶中看到美,从毁灭中明白生命,从残酷中懂得爱。

痛苦令人难过,我曾经历过悲伤和痛苦的生活,在苦难中不忘初心是不易的。

仇恨燃烧我的眼泪,泪水只为爱流淌。

山叔经历过许多事情,并不全都明白,但这就是生活。

我把真爱深埋心底,为了生存和胜利,我仇恨我哭泣我挣扎。

I am a fighter of fate in fire, in another side I am a flower under the sunshine and water with love. I feel I am as a gladiator in a colosseum at home. But not living, not dying.

As I read your words I feel your struggle, I feel your anger, and I feel your desperation... The Gardener will tend to your wounds with love and affection and his tears at your sadness will feed you. You are in a storm at the moment, but one day the sun will come out for you...

I am in the storm but I am rooted in the Mountain and Gardener always by my side plus Bear, I get more than what I lost.

我是烈火中与命运搏斗的斗士，我是慈爱中沐浴阳光的花朵，而在这个家中我是斗兽场中的角斗士，生死不明。

当我读你的文字可以感到你的挣扎，你的愤怒你的绝望。

园叔会以仁爱之心为你疗伤，他为你的伤心所留下的眼泪将抚慰你，养育你。你正经历着暴风骤雨，但太阳一定会向你露出笑脸。

我身处险境，却根植深山，园叔不离不弃，还有熊大爷。我因祸得福。

With the Mountain the Flower can relax to be beautiful.

I would gaze upon such a flower, and inhale its exquisite perfume.

Gardener and Flower will always try to make beautiful art and find a way to share it… I see Bear is an aesthetic Bear.

I think the Bear reacts to a sense of beauty. It has a love of beauty but being a wild creature it finds it difficult to intellectualise its feelings as it responds to emotion and sensation.

I always sleep naked.

Is that the Mountain, Gardener or Bear? I think with clothes he is the Gardener, once half naked he is the Mountain, once totally naked he is the Bear…

依靠着山叔， 蔷薇安静地开放。

我愿意凝视着她，深深地嗅着她细腻的芬芳。

园叔总是设法让他的蔷薇美得像艺术品。

连熊爷爷都那么有品味呢！

人家熊爷有充分的美感，它不是用语言而是用情感表达感受。

我一直都裸睡。

裸睡， 山叔园叔还是熊爷？园叔穿睡衣， 山叔半裸，熊爷全裸。

You are like a Firework, exploding at the touch of a match...

For now put the Firework in a box, where the match can't reach it... I will try my best to calm down and forget about anger.

Not forget it, control it.

I think a good way is for the Gardener to come to water the Firework as well as water the Flower, both of them need water.

Lots I think.

So leave the Flower and throw out the Firework.

The Firework is part of who you are...
You just need to control it.
The Gardener will help you, with lots of water to begin with...

I will try to keep Gardener not too tired, not to hold bigger bucket, small one is better for him, just enough to dampen the fire, not to put it out. Yes, that also from my heart, my feeling.

你就像一个炮仗一点就着。

从现在起，把它藏在一个火柴够不着的铁盒里。我会尽力冷静息怒并忘掉它。

不是忘掉是控制它。

我想到一个好办法，让园叔去给炮仗和蔷薇都浇水，因为它俩都需要。

想了很多。

相忘于江湖。

一点就着是你性格的一部分，你需要的是学会制怒。园叔会准备充足的水来帮你。我尽量别让园叔提个大桶累着，只要能抑制火焰蔓延的一小桶水就好。不谋而合。

I do want to have a big change in my life after today. I have to keep calm to be a beautiful flower, to be wet as a firework. From today I can be calm, Chinese face still.

Those that love you can see your true beauty, inside and out.... I have always seen it... And known it to be true.

In the deep of my heart I hide the real love.

That is nature, the sun sets, so the Gardener and the Mountain need to have a rest and sleep. The sun rises, the Mountain wakes up with a smile and the Gardener comes to the blooms to say hello. The new day starts.

从今往后我要改变自己的生活状态，我要做一朵安静的小花，一个哑炮仗。从现在起，保持冷静，扳起一张威严的脸。

想想那些由里到外真实的美。

我一直想着，它们是那样的真实。

真爱深藏。

这是自然规律，日落时，山叔园叔要休息睡觉前，日出，山叔微笑着醒来，园叔像花儿问早安，新的一天开始啦！

I am yearning back to the era of the Milk Lady. I thought to wear the skirt and wear scarf the arms are strong for milking. We should break the rule, convention always limits our imagination.

We can do anything, rules are to be broken, convention defied, and we are only tied by our own inhibitions.

Yes, we can try.

我渴望回到挤奶姑娘的时代，想象着自己穿着长裙戴着头巾挽着袖子，用一双粗壮的手臂挤奶。

我们应该打破成规。

惯例抑制人们的想象力。

没有什么不可能，打破成规旧俗，像传统挑战，唯一束缚我们的是我们的头脑。

是的， 我们可以尝试。

Bear can be very soft and nice, water can make Flower bloom and keep Firework calm, the sword can be hard and shiny but also can be feather.

Bear is a wild creature and can get excited.

In convention Bear is a wild creature, in creation Bear can be teddy. My Bear is a big Bear with arms to hold you close and tight.

The Mountain, the Gardener and the Bear are here for you.

I am so lucky having a powerful Mountain, sweet Gardener and an aesthetic Bear…

熊爷十分温柔善良。水使蔷薇成长，让炮仗安静。剑，既坚韧锋利又如一叶羽毛。

熊爷具有它野性的一面。

从生物学角度，熊爷具有野性，从创作性上说，它是泰迪。

这个熊爷有一双巨大的手臂可以紧紧护住你。

山叔园叔和熊爷为你保驾护航。

我是多么的幸运，有身强力壮的山叔，温和善良的园叔，和一个美感的熊爷。

It's time to sleep and keep energy for the day, naked beneath the sheets.

Freedom and unlimited, good to imagine.

It is, very good, enjoy your freedom.
Can you? Enjoy your freedom?

I can't.

I will try to help you.

睡觉了，养精蓄锐才能精力充沛，我的裸体躲在被单下。

自由自在无拘无束天马行空。

对，好啊！享受自由吧，你？你会享受自由吗？

我没有自由。

我会帮你的。

April 2016

2016年4月

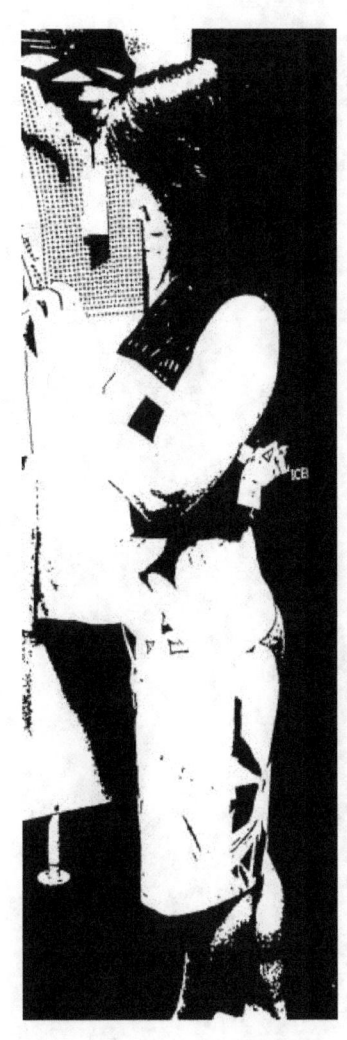

I understand what you mean by beautiful, that it includes nature and harmony. Within the anger and peace, Firework and Flower, calm down and explore.

Sorry, this old man fell asleep whilst chatting to beauty.

That old man, no sorry like you said. Just have a good sleep. Even the Mountain and Bear have to have enough rest to support the flowers. Have a nice dream.

我明白你所说的美，它包含大自然与和谐。

愤怒与平和，炮仗与蔷薇，沉默与爆发。

抱歉，谈着美却睡着了，我老了。

就像老了的你说的，不需要抱歉，晚安吧，即使是山叔熊爷也需要养精蓄锐才能精力充沛保护弱小啊。

好梦。

If there is sand in your eye or there is a fish bone in your throat, that is feeling.

I always step on the way where there seems to be no way. Yet after all of the bad things that happened to me at times, I still believe in love, trust and honesty, I still keep my dream, which means I live for my dream.

Art comes from emotion and passion, good and bad; it's about channelling the emotion into the work.

You have a good sleep, Bear, Gardener and Bear, and Mountain.

Two bears. Hehe.

I give them big hugs and lots of love, two Bears double sweets.

那感觉就像眼中柔沙， 如鲠在喉。

我总是在困境中前行，历经磨难，我依然尊崇爱，
信任和诚实。我为了自己的梦想而活。

艺术来源于情感与激情，无论快乐与悲伤，艺术将情感转化为
作品。

你睡个好觉，熊爷， 园叔，熊爷和山叔。

两只熊， 呵呵。

给他们巨大的拥抱和深爱。两只熊加倍甜蜜。

I think about the deeper meaning, that nothing materialistic is ready when we own them. Like clothes, we just use them as we think about the relationship of living and dying.

I suppose all clothes are like that, but we do try to use clothes to enhance how we look. We like the effect to be aesthetically pleasing to the eye. Bears of course don't wear clothes.

Most of us care about the body more than soul and spirit. Most people don't care about how the soul looks and what we should feed it; we care about how our body and face look like and what clothes we should wear, yes to please eyes.

Our own eyes as well as those of others.

我想，我们从没拥有任何物质上的一切，比如衣服，我们只是暂时的利用它，如果你从生死的角度去考虑。

我觉得衣服的意义正在于此，它的作用在于我们从外表上看上去怎么样，追求的是视觉上的愉悦。

当然，奥莫洛斯（amorous bear）是不需要衣服来装扮的。

大多数人重视身体而忽视灵魂与精神。他们不关心灵魂的长相和营养。人们关心自己的脸蛋儿和身材是否能取悦于人。

关心我们自己和他人的看法。

Mountain sleeps from dusk to dawn, Gardener wakes at dawn to check on his blooms, Bear wakes when aroused... Or hungry...

Then what are the results of the work of the Gardener? How hungry the Bear? How strong is the Mountain when he wakes up at dawn?

The Gardener is sad that sometimes his blooms can be damaged when he is not able to watch them, but he hopes he can do enough... The Bear can be aroused by beautiful blooms, and he is often hungry... The Mountain is a mountain, always strong, whether asleep or awake.

This is why we need gardeners for the blooms, but the wild one can never really be damaged, the harsher the condition of living, the tougher it grows, the more beautiful and strong of colour.... Like a flower dark in the night, a goddess amongst blooms. The Bear loves these blooms; The Bear sniffs the blooms.

忙叔从黄昏睡到黎明。园叔一起来就去看他的园子，奥叔被饿醒了。

园叔的园子怎么样了？奥叔饿得要紧吗？黎明时分的忙叔元气大增吧！

园叔有时真的难过因为无力保护自己的花园尽管他尽力而为了，奥叔在饥饿中被美丽的花园唤醒，而忙叔就是忙叔，无论何时都那么强壮。

所以，园叔的工作很重要，然而，风野中的玫瑰从不会被摧毁，润物细无声。

是黑暗中的夜玫瑰，是花之女神。

奥姆洛斯深深地嗅着它的芬芳。

I wrote my diary in a calm and peaceful mood. While I was writing I thought as well... Yes, when you are writing you experience words. It is the time you have wasted for your flower that makes your flower so important.

Mountain has been to the cinema, which must have been a huge cinema to fit the size. Hehe.

Yes, had to ask everybody else to leave to fit it in, then as the Gardener tried to watch the film, the Bear ran off and ate all the ice cream...

They are just the pieces of information like a fast food, same as what you said earlier, part of the deconstructed post-modernist way of relating to people in many different ways...

Yes, more and more deconstructed, we use it to relate to art.

We used to relate to pictures in galleries, books etc. Now we have an infinite number of pictures at the press of a button brought into the palm of your hand. You think of something and there it is. But it is also giving you ideas, some of which you share with other people to create dialogue, which creates more ideas, and so on.

I prefer the deconstruction way, as we experience life every day, we needn't learn from a book how to live. We create our own life, the art is hidden in the part we can't plan, such as the Mountain planned to go to the cinema today, but the Bear went to eat ice cream while the Gardener watched the film... Maybe there was no strawberry so he tried flower flavour; he found that is cool...

我现在以平和平静的心情写日记。写作是思考的过程。

是啊，写作是经历文字。

你在小玫身上花费的时间是那么的重要。奥先生嗅着玫瑰的芬芳。

山叔看电影去了。哦，那得是多大的电影院啊。

对啊，叫其他人都离开才行呢。园叔专心看电影，奥先生去吃冰淇淋了。

只是快餐文化，就像以前说的后现代解构主义。讨论在不同方面人之间的关系。

是的，越来越多的解构。

我们习惯于艺术，我们习惯于画廊里的图片和书籍。

当今，我们有无限多的图片，主要你轻触按钮就能看到你想要的。

你想到什么，它们就呈现在那里。

然而，它也带给你想法，有些想法通过对话，与他人分享，创造出更多的想法。

我喜欢解构主义方式，因为我们每天在经历着生活，我们没必要向书本学习如何生活，我们创造自己的生活。

艺术是无法在日常生活中去计划的。就如山叔今天计划去看电影，园叔专注于电影，奥先生去吃冰淇淋。

因为没有草莓口味的，他要了玫瑰味的，他发现很酷。

The Flower woke up few times during the night, she didn't see the Gardener, so she kept sleeping till now, but she wrote down a poem when awake at midnight.

No Matter
Zaiming Wang (2016)

No Matter the clothes or the house
We are just staying inside temporarily
We never have them as we thought we had
My heart lives in a Mountain
But I just show you a Flower
Both of them need neither clothes nor a house.
Natural, naked and beautiful.

夜里，小玫惊醒了几次，没见园叔。她就又睡了直到现在，不过半夜醒来她写了首诗：

无论如何
王再鸣（2016年）

不论衣服还是房子
我们只是暂居
我们从未
如想象的那样
拥有它们

我的心在山巅
我却只是
向你
敬献玫瑰

它们不需要
衣服和房屋

自然，裸露，美丽

I woke thinking about raincoat pictures as a symbol of the relationship between human beings and nature. The weather is always tough and cold but people are used to it and cope with it in their own way. No matter how cold and how hard the weather, women still have their little dresses on under the raincoat.

At beginning I think of taking the pictures in the rain, then I am thinking unnecessary, can make hair wet, wear under the hood. The style is what I am looking for, the loose hood and sense of falling. The coat falling open and loose, I am not falling as I am on the Mountain.

Once I passed the field looking at the low old stone wall, it felt close to my heart. The low wall seems to hide a lot of stories and reminds you about 'a long time ago', as you stand behind it and in front of it.

醒来时，我想着穿雨衣的照片，它是人与自然之间象征。气候总是那么恶劣，人们以自己的方式适应它。无论气候如何寒冷，女人依然在雨衣之内穿上精致的连衣裙。

开始我想要在雨中拍这些照片，然而我又想，没必要啊，把头发打湿带上连衣帽。这是我想寻找的风格，宽松的连衣帽，向下垂的感觉。雨衣下垂宽松。我不会下落因为有山托着。

每当我经过荒原，看着老旧的石墙，觉得特别亲切，低石墙似乎藏着说不尽的故事，徘徊上下听见那久远的往事。

Helping you to achieve your dream is very important for me...

You are the real Mountain, you understand me deeply.

Your beauty and inner strength were always there, I've just tried to help you see it, believe it, be it...

It is life; it teaches us and makes us become stronger and stronger. Everything I am doing is for happiness and freedom of heart, my heart is in prison, because it is not happy all the time and under big pressure.

希望你能 实现自己的梦想，这对我也很重要。

你是深深理解我的忙叔。

我只是来帮助你看见你自己的美和内在恒久的坚韧，相信你自己，成为你自己。

生活的磨难使我们越挫越勇。

我为心灵的快乐和自由而活。

可是现在我的心像一个囚徒，是那样的不快乐，还承受着巨大的压力。

Mountain, Gardener and Bear's garden is mess as they were absent at night, the flowers were drunk.

Wonderful.

Every night is different in the garden, who knows... I am working on life deeply, I feel I just follow my feelings every day. I do like my face through your lens; I think the reason comes from the power of Mountain, Gardener and Bear (MGB).

MGB get their power from the Yellow Flower, without which the images do not exist...

So both link with each other?

Absolutely.

I am looking for that feeling; strong to deal with fate and strong to create the art life.

You will find it.

I feel it so.

忙叔他们今晚不在，花园乱成一团， 花都蔫了。

太好了！

每晚的花园都不同，谁知道呢？我每天跟着感觉生活，我真的很喜欢你镜头里面自己的脸，我想原因就是忙叔们的力量。

忙叔们的力量来自于野玫瑰，没有她影像也就不存在了。

二者相互依存。

绝对是。

我又在找感觉，把强烈的与命运抗争的感觉和创造一个艺术生命的感觉。

你会的。

我会的。

Good morning, Mountain, Gardener and Bear, the blooms need watering, to be appreciated and to be rooted in the earth of Mountain. It is a holiday time coming, plus it is the season of blooming, it is the right time to see them after a long time caring for the seeds and plants. All the seasons are important but spring is the highlight. It is the time to show the Flower's dream to the people who didn't see.

MGB, have a good rest, thanks for coming and bringing a lot of sunshine and watering the Flower. It is the blooms' time, life is difficult this is why I need my Mountain, Gardener and Bear with me.

早安，忙叔们。花园需要浇水了，怀着感恩的心深深扎根于山中。

假期到了，也正是花开的时节，园叔看着自己长时间精心看顾，从种子到发芽开花的花园。四季各有千秋，但春天是花儿向世人宣告自己梦想的好时节。

忙叔们，好好休息吧。谢谢你们带来灿烂的阳光和充足的水分。生活很困难，但花儿照样开放，这是为什么我们需要忙叔们。

Good morning, the Bear awoke early this morning... I think he was dreaming about the Flower...

I see the Bear cares about the Flower more than Gardener or in a different way as the Flower is beginning to bloom.

We talked about pressure and potential, now I understand how important the Gardener is, as his watering and inspiring is important to the condition of the blooms. The Gardener has to be very confident in his flowers, and then he has to understand how to plan.

The Gardener has every confidence in his flowers, especially the little Yellow Flower opening as a Firework; it is very special to him....

I understand the meaning of Mountain, Gardener and Bear for me. The Bear can eat the flowers, but the flowers will come again and again.

The sheep and cow eat grass but Bear eat flowers. Next time the Milk Lady will feed cow.

I will look forward to that... What flowers should the Bear eat?

As they open, the yellow flowers.

早安,奥莫洛斯醒得早,他梦见了小黄。

哦,奥莫洛斯比园叔更关心花园,或许是以不同的方式吧。正是花开时节。

我们谈到压力与潜力,现在我明白了个叔多么重要,有他精心照料,才保证繁花似锦。他对自己的花园胸有成竹。

园叔很有信心,尤其是小黄像只爆竹的时候,那是他的紧急援助关头。

我明白忙叔们对我意味着什么,奥叔饿急了的时候可能会把花给吞了,可它会春风吹又生。

牛羊吃青草,奥叔吃鲜花。下次挤奶姑娘会记着给奥叔喂食。

我期待着,奥莫洛斯会吃什么呢?开放的,黄色的。

Good morning, has Bear had a sweet dream? Miss my Gardener and Mountain!

Good morning, I think the Bear has many sweet dreams.

The Gardener is very proud of the way the yellow flowers are opening and blooming. And the Mountain is a mountain, big and solid and very happy that the Yellow Flower is rooted in his side...

The weather in England is not just a topic; it is the Warriors wearing the armour, becoming a part of the personality of the English with the joy of prevailing against the bad weather.

This is why we created the raincoat pictures. I like your idea; it becomes one with the picture, a description and meaning.

早安,奥莫洛斯做了好梦吗?想念园叔和忙叔。

嗯,奥莫洛斯做了好多甜美的梦。

园叔为小黄傲雪凌霜而骄傲。忙叔用他宽广的胸襟拥抱小黄。

英格兰的天气不仅是一个话题,它是穿着盔甲和勇士与恶劣天气起舞的一场欢乐颂。

这是我们拍摄"雨衣"的原因。我喜欢这个主意。这正是照片要诠释的内涵。

Good morning MGB, I have slept once, I just lay down. I feel too heavy with this burden, the disaster of life. But I also know I have my Mountain and Gardener, oh and Bear stand by my side, so I am still a flower who blooms, a firework it is powerful to fire for dream, a sweet candy for Bear to taste. The more I feel pressure the more I feel the new life is growing up, I found this is my nature. I am encouraged by this life experience; I'd like to try many ideas with you, such as Milk Lady, Fan Dance in the ruins, fitting room pictures and sculptures. I miss old time and old personality.

I know the soul of the Flower is alive, I see it in you, I read it in your words, I feel it in me...

In another way I feel excited that we are walking on the journey of art solidly. I can see myself from the pictures you took, more confident, more meaning. I know we will fulfil our dream... I can't wait to fulfil our dream, everyday everything I did, and I do, is to clear my way to the future. I have to walk out from dark to the bright.

Yes, never stop, art is unlimited same as life.

Once I think about art I feel life flowing, but once I came back to my reality my feelings go to dark.

Of course, reality is heavy for you at the moment, and reality is where and how we live our lives everyday...

各位早安。我刚才睡了一小会儿，现在才躺下。生活的苦难使我觉得太沉重了。但同时让我更加感到你们在我身边的力量。我还是那朵野玫瑰，那支在梦中燃烧的烟花，奥莫洛斯喜爱的糖果。这生命中的磨难让我九死一生，凤凰涅槃。

我还有许多想法希望与你去尝试，挤奶姑娘，废墟上的扇舞，试衣间和陶塑。我充满怀旧情愫。

从你的文字，从你自己，我能感觉到野玫瑰灵魂的生生不息。

我很兴奋，我们正在生命中探索艺术。从你的照片里我反观自己，更加自信更多思索。我知道我们能实现这个目标。

每一天的生活都为这个目标。我必须从黑暗中走出来。

不要停步，艺术如同生命，永无止境。

当我想到艺术，生命在流动，但目前的现实又让我黯然无光。

当然，目前你的处境很沉重。现实生活就是我们所处的状态以及如何去过每一天。

Good morning, The Bear is awake early this morning...
The Mountain is silently snoring...
And the Gardener is stirring...

Good morning MGB, it seems all are in order...

You have many names, Little Yellow Flower, Yellow Flower, Firework, Little Firework, Milk Lady and Sword Warrior. And perhaps a sweet candy for the old Grey Bear...

Yes, this is the way I am thinking and doing in my life. I have written to you that once we start living by the way we think, the art is beginning from there. Thanks for all three for your good job on the Flower. She is blooming, she will be stronger, she will flame the sky not just break out for short time...

早安,奥莫洛斯今天醒得很早,忙叔还在打呼噜,园叔睡眼惺忪。

早安各位,好像各就各位了。

你有好多名字了,小黄,小玫,爆仗,小钢炮,挤奶姑娘,剑侠。还有,哈哈,老灰熊的糖果。

是啊,它们是我生活的写照。记得我曾跟你说过,我们正开始过艺术的生活。感谢各位为小玫的成长呕心沥血。她正茁壮成长,她不会昙花一现。

The Flower blooms brighter every day. Any point can become end or start according to how you decide.

You are very sweet, strong, but sweet as well.

Why and how?

Your strength and sense of purpose is there to see, for anyone who looks. But you also have a lovely sweet nature.

I see, let me think... Sense of purpose is good thing, I think. As I have never had a safe life as a woman, I have to be strong, but my nature is feminine.

It's who you are.

It's from my life experience and nature of heart. Yes, I want to create with my own life experience, live my way.

As you should, free to make your own choices...

I am a sensitive person.

I see this, I feel this, and you have so many talents.

Talent is not good as I can't control my temper, easy to be Firework.

It is part of who you are.

Yes, it is.

You have a right to be angry when someone is not honest with you...

花儿每天都在成长。每一个时刻都是终点也是起点，取决于你如何定义。

你很可爱也很坚强，但是很可爱。

为什么？

你的坚韧和目标感显而易见。但你又有着可爱的天性。

噢，让我想想，目标感是好事，作为一个女人，我从来没有安全感，我并非天生刚强。

你是你自己。

我的人生经历和内心体验造就了我，我渴望有着自己的人生道路。

你有选择的自由。

我很敏感。

我看见也感觉到了。你有能力。

有能力？我无法克制自己，一点就着。

这是你个性的一部分。

是啊。

当有人背叛你时你有权愤怒。

How is Bear? Has he had a good dream last night?

He always sleeps well and has lovely dreams, He is a happy Bear.

He is, always, how lovely is his dream?

Very lovely, full of sweet things to eat and love, but he only eats and loves the very sweetest

How he knows?

He has an aesthetic sense; he loves the exotic oriental blooms.

So, the Gardener should work hard to make the blooms stronger every day, the Bear will then see the beautiful Flower and sweetest smile, but she should be free to make her own choices; she doesn't have to allow herself to be eaten.

She does, she is nice to the nice people, but keep a distance is another way to keep long friendship.

I understand the thinking, but I think friendships are built on lots of things and aren't the same for all friends.

There is always mutual respect and understanding.

At the moment the Flower has enough to think about, and doesn't need to worry about the big old Grey Bear, he will always be here for her, no matter what.

He loves the Yellow Flower and sets no conditions for that love. His love is freely given.

I agree and understand what you said about real friends and friendship.

奥先生好吗？他昨晚做梦了吗？

他总是做着美梦醒来。他是一只快乐熊。

对，他是。说说怎么个美法？

非常美，有许多甜美的东西吸引着他，但他会选择最美妙的事儿。

他怎么知道？

他有美感，他喜欢东方情调。

那么，园叔得要每天努力工作让花园枝繁叶茂。奥先生就能欣赏最美的笑容如花绽放。美丽的花有权选择保护自己的。

没错，善有善报，但好朋友应该是"距离产生美"。

我明白，真正的友情基于许多因素。那些因素并非适用于普遍意义上的朋友。

目前小玫要考虑的太多，不必理会老奥，他永远是那个最好的朋友。

他关爱小玫，他的爱是无条件和无私的。

我同意也明白你所说的真正的朋友和友情。

It is very low moment for me, I need a rope to grab, but I am clear brained, I try to swim by myself and am thankful to all the people that are nice to me. I don't worry about the Grey Bear; he has a Red Bear by his side that cares about him.

A Red Bear?

You know, maybe a Red Lion,

A Red Lioness?

Yes, she is the leader of the pack, but she also has her dreams to follow... She knows and understands that the MGB loves and admires the blooms, and cares for them...

Red Lionesses are beautiful and powerful, they live on different sides of the Mountain, and their needs are different and change from time to time...

The Gardener works hard to care for them when needed and the Bear loves them, some are in the past and some are in the present...

这一刻我非常低落，我需要一根救命稻草。但我脑子很清晰，我努力挣扎，我衷心感谢那些善待我的人。我不担心灰熊，他有红熊在身边关爱他。

红熊？

你明白，红狮？

红雌狮？

是的，她是头儿，但她有着自己的梦想，她明白和理解忙叔们对小玫的心愿和关爱。

红雌狮很美很强壮。她在山那边。随着时间的变化她们的要求也在变化。

当她们需要时园叔尽力照顾和关爱她们，不论过去还是现在。

I am in the bus back home now. Red is lighter than purple, everywhere Red Lionesses on the mountain, hope Yellow Flower is only one for Gardener then.

Very few Lionesses left on the mountain now, and only one Yellow Flower.

That is jealous.

Are you really jealous?

That is nature I think, but I know who I am, you are my special friend post-modern way.

我在回家的公车上,红色比紫色浅,山上到处是红母狮,但愿小玫就一个。

山上只剩下几只母狮子了, 小玫只有一个。

只是在嫉妒。

你真的在嫉妒?

这是本性,但我了解自己。你是我特殊的朋友,后现代主义朋友。

Big hugs and kisses to Bear and Gardener.

Gardener and Bear have big smiles on their faces.

How about the Mountain then?

The Mountain is a mountain; he is being cool and happy.

Happy without kisses?

Does a mountain have a mouth?

No, it has a heart no mouth.

Mountain has big heart.

Oh very big, big enough for Red Lionesses running.

Not forgetting the beautiful Yellow Flower rooting.

The Yellow Flower is a part of the Mountain, an important part.

Without Yellow Flower we don't call it your Mountain, maybe Red Lionesses' Mountain.

It's my Mountain, the Red Lionesses are not jealous creatures, and aren't always on the Mountain.

大大的拥抱和亲亲奥先生与园叔。

他们开心地笑了。

那忙叔呢？

忙叔，哈，他酷酷的很快乐。

没有亲亲也很快乐？

忙叔有嘴吗？

没有，他有一颗心没有嘴。

忙叔有一颗宽广的心。

嗯，非常宽广，足够红母狮满山遍野地奔跑。

他没忘记植根于山中的小玫。

小玫是大山的一部分，重要的一部分。

没有小玫的话，也就不称之为"你的山"，那是红狮山。

是我的山，红狮不嫉妒，也不常在山里。

Nice match colour.

Not sure what you mean?

I mean grey and yellow, I feel glad to think about the Bear now.

Good.

And think of Purple Lioness in the meantime, she is the Queen, still we vote for her.

Thank you.

The Queen is purple, so who are the Red Lionesses?

Others

I am Yellow Flower belong to garden. I am keener on Bear now.

The Bear will be happy.

How about the Queen then?

She is busy being the Queen and writing.

So the Bear wants to be free to do something?

The Bear is free to do many things.

I thought the Gardener is free to do art things to make Flower bloom, not Bear's duty, Mountain is caring the Lionesses, red or purple.

That could be true.

颜色很般配。

不清楚你说什么呢。

我说灰色与黄色很搭配。想到奥先生时感到很高兴。

很好。

同时也想到了紫狮,我们还是选她当皇后。

谢谢。

皇后是紫狮,那么红母狮呢?

担任其它职务。

我是园中的黄玫,我热爱奥先生。

那皇后呢?

她忙着呢,担任皇后兼写作。

嗯,奥先生想自由自在做些事情?

奥先生自由地做了许多事情。

我想,园叔看管花园,奥叔休息,忙叔照顾母狮,红母狮紫母狮。

没错。

I'm thinking I am a Red Firework; a beautiful one, and powerful one.

Yes.

Dangerous as well.

I think so.

So I should be thinking again.

About what?

About safety.

The Firework is dangerous needs the safety facility. The Gardener has two duties, one is watering the blooms, another one is to extinguish at any time. I just worry about the water, is not enough for both, so I have to think about the Firework, should be able calm down itself.

我是一只红爆竹,一只大能量的爆竹。

是的。一只危险的爆竹。

是的。所以我要再想想。

想什么?

安全问题啊。

爆竹是危险物品,需要安全存放。

园叔现在有两个职责,一是按时给花浇水,二是随时准备灭火。我担心水不够用。我希望爆竹能自己安静下来。

Does the passion of the Bear make the Firework more dangerous?

No, passion is always beautiful, the Firework is passionate as well but it can be too excited many times; to be in isolation is good way to be safe. I think about Bear's duty for Queen.

The Queen is an important part of the lives of MGB, but she has her own dreams and so the Bear is often free to roam.

As for the Firework, the safety facility is to isolate it, leave her alone.

Do you mean completely?

Who completely, Bear or Firework?

Do you mean isolating the Firework?

The Bear is a good Grey Bear, like to keep him busy. Keep Firework humid not dry.

The Grey Bear likes to be busy.

Bear with Firework is okay, strong and dangerous. Bear is loving Bear...

Bears are always dangerous.

Red Firework is dangerous as well, so working together is good to create new things, is a good combination.

奥先生的激情会加重爆竹的危险吗？

不会，激情是美好的，爆竹也充满激情。但很多时候她会过于激动，把她藏起来会比较安全。我在考虑奥先生对于皇后的职责。

皇后是忙叔们生活的重要组成部分，但皇后有自己的梦想，奥先生经常自由自在的游荡。

至于爆竹，安全起见，把她藏起来。

你是说完全的？

谁？奥先生还是爆竹？

他喜欢忙忙碌碌，他愿意帮助爆竹处于安全状态。

奥先生喜欢忙忙碌碌。

奥先生与爆竹相处还行，强烈而危险。可爱的奥先生。

奥先生的本性是危险的。

红爆竹也是危险的。所以二者相结合有助于发明点新花样。到是一个不错的组合。

Gardener is making tea for the Queen.

The Gardener waters the Flower, Mountain roots it, the Bear works with Firework for art.

Bear is making tea for Queen.

Bear is making tea for Queen, very big mess now…

No mess, simply making tea, and then he will water the Flower…

Gardener making the tea, Bear talking to Firework.

Yes, this is what I mean; mess. Gardener water Flower, Bear make tea, Mountain care for all.

Perfectly normal on the Mountain.

园叔在给皇后准备午饭。

园叔给山中花园浇水，奥先生与爆竹交流艺术。

奥先生在准备午饭。

奥先生在准备午饭？乱套了......

不乱，简单准备午饭，然后浇花。

园叔准备晚饭，奥先生与爆竹交谈。

对呀，我就是这个意思！什么乱七八糟的园叔浇花奥先生煮饭忙叔统筹。

山中井井有条。

Mountain tries to be a safe place. Gardener tries to care for and encourage everyone on the Mountain. The Bear is a bear, he is an artist, a traveller, a lover, and he is many things.

Gardener is off to water the Yellow Flower. Bear is making breakfast.

The Flower is out; Gardener will water her when she returns. She is flying to release the Firework.

Dangerous?

The Firework is calm and more safe now and going home…

忙叔是个安全的避风港，园叔关心和鼓励每一个在港中的人。奥先生，他是一个艺术家，一个旅行者，一个情人，他身兼数职。

忙叔下班了，给花园浇水来了。奥先生现在任厨师准备早餐。

小玫不在，园叔等她回来给她浇水，她像鸟一样飞去帮助爆竹了。

危险吗？

爆竹释放后安全了，冷静下来回家了。

The Bear is looking for the Yellow Flower and his paw is for protection. I mean Bear cares for the Flower and looks at it. Oh his paw is going to touch... I like the Bear looking at Yellow Flower.

Especially for you.

I see. I like my special Bear then.

奥先生在找黄玫，用他的力量保护她。我是说奥先生想要关心照顾小玫。随时保护她。

我很开心他关心她。

是的，单单为了她。

嗯，对我来说奥先生是那么的特别。

The Rat thinks he is attractive man to Chinese women for sex... But I am not so keen; I can see I am a sexually cold person.

I don't see you as a sexually cold person.

I am with him... Maybe my sex is just for real love.

I think inside you are a sensual woman...
And when it is right for you, it will be wonderful.
You just need to feel love, from someone who loves you for who you are, not for what they can get out of you.

In my life I never feel true love, I always fight against fate.
And I am very saddened about the sex part.

那只老鼠以为他很性感对中国女人很有吸引力。我不以为然，我性冷淡。

我不认为你是性冷淡的人。

与那只老鼠在一起...也许我没遇到真爱。

我认为你内心充满性感。

如果遇到真爱你也很性感。你需要感受到真爱，一个真正爱你的人爱的是你本人。而不是他希望中的你。

我一生从未遇见真爱，我总是在与命运抗争，我非常伤感于性。

This night I turn my head from hate to love, look at the nice Grey Bear longingly.
Although the Queen is there looking at me,
I kiss him in heart...

The old Grey Bear is tired and falling asleep...
Maybe the company of the Yellow Flower, will make him feel young again...

You are more than my friend.

I know, and you are more than my friend, 'special friend' post. I say good night sweet dreams as you are happy one.

I like that... The Bear is happy.

今晚我的心化干戈为玉帛。看着充满渴望的奥先生，尽管皇后在看着我，我在心里亲吻了他。

老奥莫洛斯累了，沉沉地睡了。

也许有小玫陪伴。

让他觉得又年轻了。

你不仅仅意味着朋友。

我知道，你是特殊的朋友。因为你总是快乐的所以我说晚安好梦。

这个我喜欢，快乐的奥先生。

I wrote this when Bear fall asleep just now.

I know I read them, beautiful words, thank you.

The words from my heart, my words just follow my heart.

In this Midnight
Zaiming Wang (2016)

In this midnight,
Lonely and scared as dawn still far,
In the dark,
I saw the light from the eyes of the Grey Bear,
It is my Bear
A Bear with blue eyes
Grey Bear with blue eyes
I will remember the blue eyes.

Looking at you with love, respect and honesty, respect and honesty is rock and root for love.

在奥先生沉睡的时候我写了这个。

我知道，我读了，美好的文字，谢谢你。

这些文字发自内心，它们表达我的心声。

在这个午夜
王再鸣（2016年）

在这个午夜
孤绝而恐惧
因为黎明还远

在黑暗中
我见到
一束光
从奥莫洛斯
蓝色的眼睛里
闪现出来

带着关爱看着你，尊重与真诚，尊重与真诚是爱的牢固的基石。

Good morning, the Bear still awake or go to sleep again?

No, Bear is awake now.

Good morning Grey Bear, do you have a sweet dream?

Yes, very sweet...

Sounds Grey Bear was happy in his dream.
The Yellow Flower has no feeling now, just worry.

I understand about the Yellow Flower's feelings, the Grey Bear just woke up and was still dreaming...

The battle should be stopped and I deserve to have a time of peace to think about our art and my little sculptures. The Yellow Flower does want to be rooted in the Mountain in England.

I know and the Mountain wants you here, the Yellow Flower is beginning to bloom so beautifully.

In my experience the more honest you are with people, the more they understand you. I think this particularly true with women...

Indeed totally true, honesty is the smartest way to be a great person and brave one, and the best way to love and be loved...

Yes, honesty is the one basic element for real love.

早上好，奥先生醒着还是去睡了？

没睡，他醒着呢。

早上好奥先生，做了什么好梦吗？

嗯，很美的梦。

听起来奥先生挺高兴。小玫没心情只是担心。

我理解你的感受。老奥醒的时候还在梦里呢。

这场战役应该停止了，我应该安静一下想想我们正在进行的艺术创作和我自己的小雕塑。黄玫希望扎根于忙叔所在的英格兰。

我明白，忙叔也希望小玫留在这儿，她正如花似玉。

我的经验告诉我，你越是以诚相待，越是被理解，尤其是女性。

完全正确，诚实是伟大的灵魂和勇敢者的智慧，也是爱与被爱的正确途经。

诚实是真爱的基本要素。

May 2016

2016年5月

Firework crackled for devil...

A woman is not something you can treat with tricks, a woman should be treated with respect and honesty, and she is not inferior to man. In one way the Rat has experience, to cheat, in another way he has no experience of me deeply. Once I start against him he starts to know me, Little Firework with strong mind.

I don't think he has any concept of who you are; I believe you have very deep inner beauty and strength. Spending time with you is a voyage of discovery...

Yes, the Rat will never know me; he lives in the other world.

You are a woman, a mother, a friend, a teacher, an artist, a philosopher, a writer. Stand up, you are strong, you are beautiful...

The Yellow Flowers's love is open and she smiles to her Gardener every day, she is trying.

The Gardener is delighted to see the Yellow Flower's blooms opening.

The Yellow Flower is strong, open and understands more of life and love...

爆竹被那个恶魔激怒了。

不要对女人施诡计耍花招，对女人要青眼相看，以诚相待，把持男女平等的姿态。

那只诡计多端自以为是的耗子并不真的了解我。一但我开始反击他就知道小钢炮的巨大威力。我坚信深藏的内在美的力量。

与你相处也是发现你的过程。那只耗子永远无法理解你，他活在另一个世界里。

你是一个女人，一位母亲，一个朋友，一名教师，一个艺术探索者，一个思考者，一个记录者，振作起来，你是坚强而美丽的。

黄玫的心和笑脸向园叔敞开，她在努力。

看见小玫绽放的生命之花，园叔由衷地高兴。

生命之花绽放是小玫对生命与爱深深的理解和强烈的渴望。

Yellow Flower misses Bear.

Bear dreams about Yellow Flower.

I see, now I understand the dream of Grey Bear.

Silly old Grey Bear.

He is Bear, it is nature. This Bear is a gentleman thinking of the Queen, the Yellow Flower does understand and thinking too.

What a wonderful exotic flower you are.

My heart was in prison without love for long time, I put myself in prison with a lot of reasons, I thought honest, I found that is to cheat myself, and maybe this is exotic thinking?

Possibly, but love should never be in chains.

I am in chains for one reason to another reason, so my mind is the prison of love.

Sometimes others put us in chains, sometimes we put ourselves in chains, and love should have no chains.

It is true, how do you think I can be free of the chains?

Grey Bear is not strong enough to remove all your chains but he is trying to remove those he can...

黄玫想你奥先生。

奥先生梦见了黄玫。

哦，现在我理解熊之梦了。

傻傻的...

这是人之常情。笨熊是个绅士，一直想着皇后，黄玫十分理解，也这么想。

美妙啊，散发着异国的芬芳。

我的心被长期禁锢，因为各种原因我自闭了自己。我是自欺欺人，也许这是异邦人的方式。

可能吧。但是爱是没有束缚的。

因为不同原因我将自己禁锢着，远离爱。

有时是他人强加于我们，有时是自己，爱不应该有束缚。

没错，我应该如何挣脱束缚？

奥先生无能为力帮你挣脱所有的束缚，但他会尽他所能帮你。

Beside love we have responsibility. Love has more meaning.

Grey Bear would never use chains; his love has no conditions, no expectations and is freely given.

The Grey Bear has a Queen, so my love to him includes his Queen.

And so your chains begin to fall.

I have no chain for Grey Bear and his Queen; it is my way to love.

And we have no chain for you.

So I love you both.

The Flower is blooming, and is free.

Yes, free heart and mind now, free are the wings that can make me fly, I am flying up in the sky, alone but happy…

除了爱还有责任。爱的意义是广泛的。

奥先生永远不会去束缚，他的爱无条件，不求回报，无偿给予。

奥先生有皇后，我爱屋及乌。

那么你就从束缚中解脱出来了。

我对他们的爱是自由的，这是我的爱的方式。

没有束缚。

我爱你们。

玫瑰自由绽放。

是的，身心自由。自由是翅膀，使我飞翔，我翱翔在天空中，孤独快乐。

As Yellow Flower I enjoy my Gardener's watering.

He loves watering the Yellow Flower and watching her grow.

Freedom is the way to be alone on your journey, it is the only way. She is growing, growing strong, growing freely and growing to get to know love.

She doesn't have to be alone... True friends will love her for who she is, will share the journey with her from time to time... But will never try to exploit her, or chain her...

Inside we are all alone, but a journey is less tiring, when shared with others and can be fun.

From the Mountain, Gardener and Bear only feel love, and the Yellow Flower shows her love by blooming.

黄玫享受着园叔的抚慰。

园叔热爱自己的工作，安慰黄玫，看着她成长。

自由是一个孤独的旅程，也是唯一的道路。她在自由中成长，在爱里壮大。

她不应该孤独，知心朋友理解她，愿意分享她的人生旅程，但不会利用和束缚她。

我们的内心都是孤独的，如果有了知心朋友，人生旅程就充满乐趣和动力。

对忙叔们的知遇之恩，小玫报之以李

Love has different meanings; I feel love from Grey Bear in many ways.

How many ways?

Naughty old Grey Bear...

But you are right; Grey Bear does feel love for you in many different ways...

Soul, spirit, friendship, partner of art, and some desire, I believe...

Two chains before, one left now, as for desire...

What I mean by loneliness is similar to what you say. Alone is beautiful feeling, strong and independent in mind. If strong enough inside, people can enjoy being alone.

I think so...

爱的意味不同。奥先生的爱有多重意义。

有多少重呢？

调皮的老灰熊。

没错，奥先生的爱是不同层次的。

灵魂，精神，友谊，艺术伙伴，也有些许欲望，我承认。

之前的两个束缚，现在剩下一个了。

我所说的孤独与你说的相似，孤独是美丽的，内心独立。内心必须相当强大人们才能那孤独的快乐……

我同意。

I have a poem here for the Rat.

The Game
Zaiming Wang (2016)

The game is over
Hit your road with your equipment
We will pray for you
Nightwalker.

Letting go, I feel the power of calm now.

关于耗子的一首诗。

游戏
王再鸣（2016年）

游戏结束了
用你的面具击打地面吧
我们为你祈祷
夜行者

一切过去了，我感到静默的力量。

I just want to ask if it is bed time...

Yes, I am in bed.

I see the Bear is in bed now; I am walking to the dream with free heart.

I like those words.

I am looking forward you coming back from Japan.

The Gardener will water a lot before he is absent.

The Flower will water herself and keep growing happily.

MGB will always have time for the Yellow Flower.

That's Gardener's job, he is a responsible person.

And what's the Bear's job?

Bear's job is to imagine.

Bear's job is caring for the person in need.

Sometimes Bear should be working as a fireman but seems Bears job is sleeping...

想问问上床了吗？

嗯，我在床上。

哦，奥先生也上床了。我带着自由的心进入我的梦。

我喜欢这样的文字。

我期待着你从日本回来。

园叔走之前会给花园浇足了水。

小玫会照顾好自己的。

忙叔们永远关心着小玫。

那是园叔的工作，他是一个责任心强的人。

那奥先生的工作是什么呢？

老奥是幻想家。

奥先生总是帮助有需要的人。

有时奥先生是个消防员。现在他似乎睡着了。

Bear is waking this morning...

Good morning Grey Bear, hold hand.

Kissing your hand.

Kissing beard of Bear, I feel his fur, nice and soft.

He holds you.

Nice Bear, nice hands, beautiful heart.

Nice Flower, delicate and beautiful.

Damaged, but coming back stronger.

Holding you close, feeling your heart beating next to mine.

Next to the Queen as well, you one side, she the other.

Maybe different, I think Queen in between, in between the Bear and the Flower; I respect this position very much. I understand you are always my friend in heart no matter where I am standing.

Queen is still sleeping at present.

No matter who we are together, she is awake always in my mind.

I feel the same, you are and will always be in my heart and Queen is in my heart too.

I understand.

Big hugs as you are making the tea for Queen.

奥先生一早就醒了。

早上好奥先生，握手。

吻你的手。

亲亲奥先生的胡须，我感到他的皮毛柔软而亲切。

他护着你。

可爱的奥先生，可爱的手，美好的心。

可爱娇柔的花朵。

愈挫愈勇。

紧紧搂着你，感觉你的心跳是那样的近。也紧紧倚靠着皇后，一边是她一边是你。

也许是这样，皇后在中间，一边是奥先生一边是小玫。

我非常尊重这个状态，我心里明白你是我永远的朋友，什么为位置并不重要。

皇后还睡着呢。

无论与谁在一起，她在我心里一直是醒着的。

我有同感。你总是，也将永远在我心里。皇后也在我心里。

我懂。

一个大大的拥抱给正在为皇后准备早餐的奥先生。

Flogged in Heart
Peter Lay & Zaiming Wang (2016)

How can you really understand?
The incomplete beautiful
If you didn't experience being flogged in heart
Plus the tears.

I think you can never really understand
What another person is thinking or feeling.
But you can listen to their pain,
You can see their pain,
And if you love them,
You will feel some of their pain.
You can hold them,
And be there for them...

鞭笞
彼得-雷 王再鸣（2016年）

如果不经历痛心泣血
你怎能理解残缺之美

你永远无法明白
我的心思与痛

但我可以倾听你的苦难
我能看见你流的泪

如果你爱他们
你就会痛

Good morning, did Bear have nice dream last night? It is good for Bear to sleep well and Mountain and Gardener too, they have lots of jobs they have to do, lots of love to give, a lot of dreams still to fulfil...

You show a good understanding of the Mountain, Gardener and Bear.

I think I understand MGB, they have different dreams with different desires, but with Yellow Flower, they have a great job to make her bloom with open flower.

She is a remarkable flower.

She is lucky to have such a, wonderful and understanding Gardener.

The Gardener sees the beauty and recognises the unlimited potential of the exotic bloom, a flower very rare.

As only one in this world, her experience of suffering is too heavy to bear for others. It is part of her dream she understands, she come from sky and will go back finally. Fell from sky, fly back, one more step away from the past, towards the future. No matter how hard and how difficult life is for me my heart always look towards the future, this makes me feel my present life and see the deep meaning of life from my suffering.

The past is past, and we should reflect on it and learn from it. The present is now; it is where we live our lives. How we choose to do that is for each of us to decide. The future is still to be written, some we can plan, some we can hope and some is unknown...

早上好。昨晚睡的好吗？休息好对奥先生他们很重要。因为他们工作繁忙，充满爱心，还富于梦想。

你非常理解他们啊！

我想是的。他们各自怀揣梦想。黄玫的茁壮成长便是这梦想之一。

她还不错。

她如此幸运，遇到了好伯乐。她的痛苦超出了所能忍受的程度，他人也许不能明白。她把那视为梦的一部分。尘归尘，土归土。从天空俯冲，再展翅翱翔，从过去飞向未来。曾经沧海难为水，除却巫山不是云。

失败是成功之母。我们活在当下。命运掌握在自己手里。我们对明天依然充满梦想。，明天的一切，有些可以规划，有些可以盼望，有些无法预知。

I am learning that strong is not just powerful, it is also full ability to calm down. The quiet sword, sharp and shining, I need it for my dream...

我渐渐明白,强壮并不等于有力,它还包含着以柔克刚。

静默之剑,凛凛寒光,寄托着我的梦。

I was crying a few times today, now I am in tears for your love to me.

I would kiss away your tears...

My tears were kissed away and smile now.

Holding you in my arms, I am feeling it, stroking your hair.

I can feel the soft paw is stroking my hair. The Bear paw can be very sharp and attack, in another hand he can be very soft and nice once his heart full of love.

His paw is soft against the Yellow Flower.

Yes, very soft I can see.

He is inspired by you.

I am glad to know the Grey Bear is inspired.

今天哭了好几次，这次是感动于你的爱。

我愿意吻干你的泪。

眼泪被吻去了，眼睛笑了。

紧紧拥抱着你，轻抚你的长发。

我能感到我的头发被轻抚着...
熊爪是坚利而具有攻击性的，而当他心中充满爱时，它又是那样的温柔如绵。

它们温柔地轻抚着黄玫。

小黄感受到了。

他被小玫所激励。

我很高兴奥先生被激励。

Do you sleep naked?

With a lot of clothes.

I would get so hot...

Why do you feel hot as I wear clothes?

I meant I would get hot if I wore clothes in bed.

I see, so you have to sleep naked, I think the reason is the Bear has enough hair to make him hot, no need clothes.

Yes, Bear is always naked, apart from his grey hair, if you look; Grey Bear is older so hair is not thick.

Oh that should be easy but I still have to look carefully.

Bear is happy for you to look, he likes to look at the Yellow Flower, she is a beautiful flower.

你裸睡吗？

我穿着睡。

我觉得热。

为什么我穿衣服你觉得热？

我是说如果我穿衣服睡觉我觉得热。

哦，你必须裸睡。我以为灰熊的皮毛足够温暖，所以无需再穿衣服。

奥先生一直裸睡，除了灰绒毛，岁月使我毛发稀疏，如果你细观察的话。

嗯，那就简单多了，但我还是得小心。

奥先生愿意被观看，他也喜欢看小黄，她很美。

Good morning, Bear is stretching and waking.

Oh good morning Bear; I could feel the big hugs from Bear.

Yes, his arms are around you.

I can feel it in my heart, he is a gentle Bear.

Yes, I think he is.

MGB is moving far in two days, the Yellow Flower will be blooming when he move back.

That will be so beautiful to see.

Yellow Flower will miss Gardener of course, but she becomes stronger and stronger.

Part of the Gardener's work is to help make her stronger, independent and free to choose her own destiny...

She will, she understand, she will try.

早安。奥先生抻着懒腰醒了。

哦,早安。我感到了一个大大的拥抱。

对呀,他的双臂正环抱着你。

我感动在心,温柔如奥。

是他。

忙叔们要出几天门,园叔回来后才能浇花。

黄玫会想念他们,但她足以自已。

园叔的工作就是帮助她独立,自由选择自己的命运。

她明白,她正在这样做。

MGB will miss the Yellow Flower and is already looking forward to when we will see her again.

She changed a lot of her understanding of life through this calamity, she uses own brain and experience to try to explain what is love, she just does what she thinks is correct for her dream.

Love is hard to define, it's what you feel but how you feel it is also hard to define. Your past experience and brain may be cautious but you can only let love in by opening up to it. Your dream is to find beauty in life and love through art and nature.

Yes, it is true I learnt and feel love by my experience.

忙叔们也想念小玫，总是期待着再见面。

通过这次不幸的遭遇，小玫对生活的理解有了许多改变。她用自己的生命体验诠释和理解什么是爱。这一切都是梦的一部分。

爱很难定义，关乎各人感受。而如何感受亦无定式。你的不幸使你变得谨慎，但我以为我们还是应该以开放的心态接受爱。你的梦想不正是在生命中找到美，通过艺术和自然表达爱吗！

没错，我的人生教给我什么是爱。

I have sent three small sculptures to your email; can you tell which one is me?

First one?

I think three, three are me.

Sorry, I thought one was drunker.

Yes one is drunk also is me, I am drunken Yellow Rose and you are MGB.

I really like your sculptures, they are great…

I showed the Queen the purple lion, she liked it, said she could see herself in it… However, she said she was born in the year of the tiger, so is a Purple Tigress… Queen Tiger.

我通过email给你发了三个小雕塑，你能猜出哪个是我吗？

第一个？

我想，三个都是我。

对不起，我以为其中一个是醉汉。

是的，一个是醉汉同时也是我。我是醉汉，黄玫。你是忙叔，园叔和奥先生。

我很喜欢你的小雕塑，它们很可爱。

我给皇家长看了紫狮子，她也喜欢，她说从中能认出她自己来。然而，她说她属虎，是紫虎，母老虎啊……

I feel very happy Queen Tiger liked my sculpture too; she can see herself in it! Wow! This is very encouraging to me to keep working on them, when I make Purple Tiger I just think of her picture on Facebook and imagine through your talking about her.

You were born in year of the cow then…

Really? Oh, yes the Ox.

Once I have time to make small sculpture I feel very happy and feel another part of me, I do like that. I think you should be busy sorting out for your journey to Japan.

I'm in bed now, will finish the packing tomorrow.

I see bed Bear now, bed time means naked time?

For me, yes.

Warm tonight.

Here is warm as well.

我很高兴家长也喜欢我的雕塑。她能从中认出自己，喔，这对我是巨大的鼓励。当我捏那个小人儿时，我只是想着照片中她的样子，还有通过你谈到她时。

你是属奶牛？

真的吗？哦，公牛。

每当我有空可以做小雕塑时，我非常高兴，感觉到了自己的另一部分。我真的很开心。我猜想你一定在忙着准备你的日本之行。

我在床上呢。明天可以收拾好行李。

哦，奥先生上床了，也就是说裸着了。

对我来说，是的。

今晚很热。

这儿也是。

Good morning Mountain, Gardener, Bear and Ox, longer title now, lots of hugs to all. I hope you have a good day today as you should be busy. I am going to Chinese school today.

Very long title, so good morning Yellow Flower, good morning Little Firework, hugs and kisses for all... Not forgetting drunken Yellow Flower.

I think Peter Lay is very powerful name, short simple and easy, 'lay' in Chinese is thunder, beware the powerful thunder...

This thunder is far, you only can hear his noise.

But as it comes closer, it grows dark and intimidating, oh and noisy, and then you get wet, then you have to take your clothes off to dry them...

I see, intimidating soon, that's the thunder feeling.

Yes, in a slightly scary natural way, because nature can be very powerful and beyond our control.

Yes, nature is beyond our control, so we can only respect it and understand it.

It is the smart way to be close to nature and learn from it, we will get power from it; we will be unlimited and creative.

Yes, unlimited in our imagination and creation.

早上好忙叔，公牛。头衔增加了，拥抱的需求也加大了。祝你又一个忙碌的日子快乐。我今天要去中文学校。

头衔很多。早安黄玫，小钢炮，亲吻拥抱你们，别忘了醉汉小黄。

我觉得雷彼得这个名字很震慑，短小有力。'lay'中文音译是打雷，小心雷电！

这个雷很远，你只能听见声音。

但当它接近时就变得压抑和胁迫了，还有轰响。你会湿透，于是你得脱下衣服把它晾干。

哦，来势汹汹，这是对雷电的感受。

对，自然有时叫我们畏惧，因为它可能变得强有力而超出人类的掌控。

是的，我们无法掌控大自然，我们要做的是遵循和理解自然法则。

亲近自然向自然学习才是智慧之道。从中吸取力量，我们自身变得无限和富有创造性。

对，无限的想象与创造。

I will miss you…

I will miss you too.

You are part of my life, you are my Gardener. I know I have to be stronger to make my Gardener relax. I will try when you come home so you can see the Flower open.

That would be wonderful, you are my Yellow Flower, you are the Little Firework, and you are Zaiming Wang, an artist.

Yes, I am all of them, I am always surprising.

And a sweet candy for the Bear?

Because of the Queen, the candies are bitter.

How so?

How? As I love both of them.

The Queen believes in you too… She would like to meet you.

I would like to meet her, and thank her for her understanding of our art work.

She is also an artist, mainly with words, but with drawing and painting as well… She also has had difficult times in her life… She respects our work.

Hard experience make women understand life deeply; bring the gift to them if they are strong enough.

Thanks to her for respecting our work.

我会想念你。

我也会想念你。

你已成为我生命的一部分,你是我的园丁。我也明白我必须自强,使园丁放心。我会努力,当园丁回家看见满园春色。

那太棒了,你是小黄,你是小钢炮,你是Zaiming Wang,一个艺人。

是我,我总令人惊讶。

也是奥先生的糖果吗?

因为有皇家长,糖果略带苦味。

那怎样?

怎样?因为我爱她/他们。

家长相信你,她想见你。

我愿意见她,感谢她的理解。

她自己本身就是艺术家,她舞文弄墨,也能描龙画凤。她还曾经有过痛苦的人生经历,她尊重我们的工作。

苦难使女性更深刻地理解生活,苦难是那些坚强女人的财富。

感谢家长对我们工作的肯定。

Good morning, I am so happy to know that I can inspire you. And you feel your dream when we work together. You come to me, help me with my dream, I am encouraged to start my art dream; I feel the new life beside the marriage. Now I fight as an artist, life artist to be free, get out from prison. I am not alone, I am very rich of love, I do want to win; I have to fight to win.

I believe that you and I will create something wonderful, something we are proud of...

I believe it too, I have that feeling.

I always have some time for talking with you.

Talking is nice moment of art, love, and philosophy, we can relax to think and talk about life after busy day. When I have ideas and feeling of life I write it down or fast write to you, you are my diary, but more than a words diary, I talk to you, write to you, thinking of you.

We are finding our way, much of these ideas and feelings can go into our book.

Diary is quiet and just smile to listen, you can reply and reflect, guide, water, root, hug, kiss, and a lot of things I can feel from you.

Some for the performance only we will see, your words are full of such beauty.

Thank you, I am a very sensible mind I think.

早上好。得知我可以激励你，这让我很开心。你说我们一起工作是在实现你的梦想。你是来帮助我实现梦想的，在你的激励下我开始我的艺术之梦，我感到了新的生命，与婚姻无关，现在我像个艺人一样为自由抗争，冲出牢笼。我不是弹枪匹马，我心中充满爱，我得赢，我必得胜！

我相信你我将创造一个引以自豪的未来。

我也坚信，我有预感。

我总是需要一些时间与你交流。

忙碌了一天之后，我们需要放松下来谈论和思索艺术，爱和哲学。当我对生活有感触和想法时，我喜欢写下来，或者快速地写给你。你就像我的日记本。但不单是文字上的。我与你分享，想念你。

我们有自己的方式，我们可以把其中大部分编成一本书。

"日记本"安静而面带微笑地倾听，你可以回答，反应，引导，水，根，拥抱，亲吻。我可以从你的文字感觉到好多东西。

这是你我心照不宣的语境，你的文字充满了美感。

感谢你这么说，我是个敏感的人。

You take the pictures of me to show who I am by your own way. But beside that, Gardener water the Flower, Bear comfort her, Mountain care for her very much, and Queen understanding her, All of these are love.

I do like to make sculpture. Yes, I will try to make my body or other people's, then you will become my model, I hope you will agree.

Of course I will.

You needn't worry about belly then, that is Mountain, Gardener and Bear.

Your sculpture heads have so much expression; I am really looking forward to seeing how you express the body... I am what I am, belly and all.

I have a strong feeling of the way to express your body, not very clear but I know once I start to make it the way will be there. Maybe life experience and hard struggles of sadness will help me, all those things help I think.

Can't wait to see how you express my body, and yours.

I will make your body from imagination first, I think.

That's a good idea, can't wait to see it... I hope the Fimo arrives soon.

你为我拍照，用你的方式展现我是谁。除此之外，园叔还负责打理花园，奥先生要抚慰小玫，忙叔也非常惦念她。就连家长也非常懂得小玫。这一切都充满了爱。

我真的喜欢做雕塑。我要尝试做人体，我自己或别人。我希望你能做我的模特。

当然，我会的。

你不需要担心你的肚囊，那正是忙叔园叔和奥先生。

你做的头像雕塑很有表现力。我期待着看你如何表达身体。我就是我，肚囊或者其他的。

我有强烈的感觉如何去表达你的身体。不是太明晰，但我知道，一旦我开始做，方法就在那儿了。也许生活经历和痛苦的挣扎对我有帮助，所有的生活都不是白过的。

我急不可待看你如何表达我的身体，和你自己的。

我会通过想象来做你身体的雕塑。

好主意，期待着，希望软陶泥很快就寄到了。

It's great you can text message from Japan. I feel not so far away. I can feel you are enjoying and excited by the exotic culture. You will have lots of ideas and feeling for the further steps of book and art. I am happy you are getting the fresh air and nourishment as you are Ox. I miss you Mountain, Gardener and Bear. Have a great time in Japan.

太好了，你能从日本发短信。我感到你并不遥远。可以看出你非常激动和享受异域文化带给你的感受。你将会对下一步如何做有很多好主意。我很高兴你在呼吸新鲜空气和吸取营养，因为你是公牛。我想你忙叔们，祝你日本之行愉快。

I visited the Hama Rikyu gardens, Tokyo yesterday, with my lovely friend Motoko san. The gardens were very beautiful and we enjoyed traditional Japanese tea there.

The Mountain doesn't say much but he misses the Yellow Flower, the feel of your roots and the passion of the Firework. The photographer is looking forward with excitement to capturing more of the Sword Lady through his lens as well as the beautiful blooms opening for him... The Ox is anticipating the Milk Lady and the Grey Bear still has his dreams...

The nice fragrance of plum flower is coming from the cold tough weather.

That's a Chinese poem. Another says,

It's said the Janus of sword comes from grinding.

昨天，我参观了东京的滨离宫恩赐花园，由我可爱的朋友元子女士陪同。花园无比美丽，我们在那品尝了传统的日本茶。

忙叔虽没说什么，但他很思念小玫，感受着小野花扎根于斯，和小钢炮火爆的性情。

摄影师先生殷切地期待着用他的镜头捕捉圣殿女侠如蔷薇绽放。

公牛企盼着挤奶姑娘，奥先生念念不忘他的梦想。

梅花香自苦寒来。

一句中国古诗，下句是：

宝剑锋从磨砺出。

I have got the Fimo today, I feel grateful for MGBO's love for me, and I do want to do all the things of art to match that love he gave to me. I have made the beautiful Black Lady I met, her face touched my heart. I am thinking how to make the sculpture of your body, which will be the first whole body I will try to do it. Let's see how it will be.

Wow! MGBO, my name is growing...

我今天收到了软陶泥，衷心感谢忙叔们对我的厚爱。我真心想做一切与艺术有关的事情来报答这一切。我做了一个很美的黑人妇女头像，她的脸触动我的心。我还在考虑着如何做你的人体雕塑。看看吧，会是怎样的呢……

哦，忙叔，园叔，奥先生，公牛，我的名字长长了。

Your name is growing all the time. I am really excited by the idea of my sculpture... I was trying this evening but I made the Black Lady again. I do like the Black Lady, her face, her way of talking, exciting, 58 and full of stories.

I am thinking of your body, you will see, I am excited by the thought of making it.

I just woke up, its 7:00am here, so still in bed... Tell me about the Black Woman.

She is from Uganda.

Yellow Flower and the Black Woman, from different cultures, both new in foreign lands... How does that feel? Is England the green and pleasant land of their dreams?

你的名字总在长。想到要做人体雕塑令我兴奋不已。我今晚尝试了一下，但最终我还是做了黑人妇女的头像。我很喜欢她，她的脸，她说话的方式，她的激情，她58岁充满经历和故事。

我在思索着如何做你的人体雕塑，真是令人兴奋。

我才醒，现在这里是早上7点，还在床上... 说说黑人妇女。

她来自乌干达。

黄玫与黑人妇女都是在异国他乡，来自不同的文化背景，那是怎样的感觉？英格兰是她们梦想的绿色之地吗？

Grey Bear woke up, he was dreaming about the Milk Lady... Gardener said silly old Bear, go back to sleep... Mountain thinks the Grey Bear and the Ox, both like the Milk Lady...

The Ox is asleep...

Bear smiles he loves the Yellow Flower, the Firework, the Sword Warrior and the Milk Lady.

奥先生醒了,他刚才梦见挤奶媛了。园叔说,傻老头,快回去睡觉。忙叔知道奥先生和公牛都喜欢挤奶媛。

但公牛还睡着……

傻老头笑了,他喜爱小玫,小钢炮,圣殿女侠和挤奶媛。

It is noisy, midnight in one room of the hotel in Japan, 14th May 2016. A blue eyed, naked, fat white man has a big dream, suddenly, the Ox, Grey Bear, Gardener, Mountain, the Yellow Flower, Firework, Sword Warrior, Milk Lady, all of them come out and start talking to each other,

The story is long and complex, as the relationship between all of them are mixed weirdly. They decide to communicate with each other using a special language different from the usual one.

Sometimes pleasure
Sometimes calm
Sometimes fire
Sometimes water
But they agree
With each other
In beauty and love.

By using their own language to talk, it makes understanding easier, Yellow Flower is rooted in Mountain, Gardener waters her, Firework always noisy and boom, Grey Bear tries to smile at the Flower but Firework covers it by fire smile. Ox is waiting for the Milk Lady, the big fat white man is snoring naked on the bed and the Sword Warrior is fighting for her freedom dream; they are all in the beautiful journey of art...

The Chinese woman has finally created peace and calm in the room, she is an artist... All now sleeping...

This story is becoming an epic tale that will be retold for thousands of years.

2016年5月14日，一个嘈杂的午夜，在日本一家宾馆的一间屋子里，一个蓝眼睛裸体的白胖子，做了一个长长的梦......
突然间，公牛，奥先生，园叔，忙叔，黄玫，小钢炮，女侠和挤奶媛七嘴八舌相互讨论起来。

故事很长也很错综复杂。因为他们之间的关系很不寻常。他们决定以不相通的特殊语言彼此之间进行交流。

时而兴高采烈
时而静默无语
一会儿火一般热烈
一会儿水一般清凌
但是他们对美和爱的观点始终是一致的。

他们用自己的语言谈论着，这使他们彼此易于理解。黄玫深深地藏在忙叔的心里，园叔时时看顾她，小钢炮总是叽叽喳喳，奥先生面带微笑，可她不易被驯化。

公牛在等挤奶媛，大白胖子光着身子在床上打呼噜，女侠舞枪弄剑，如梦如幻。这一切都发生在一次艺旅之中。

最后，一位中国女人使大家静了下来，突然间，所有人都平和地睡去了。

这个奇妙的故事将被世世代代讲下去。

Sword Woman
Zaiming Wang (2016)

Naked, a sword in hand,
only the honest and brave woman,
dare to calm.
She is real and beautiful,
Tears, smiling, standing,
never give up, by nature.
The water dropping from her hair,
the sword in her hand,
she will kiss by eye light.

Tears
Peter Lay (2016)

If you fall,
I will pick you up
If you cry,
I will hold you
If you smile,
I will kiss you.

剑侠
王再鸣（2016年）

一丝不挂
只求剑在握
忠诚和英勇
只为配得上静默

看她
泪眼　笑靥　挺立
以命相许
皆为梦

发尖水滴
手中剑

眼中吻

眼泪
彼得-雷（2016年）

你滑落
我以臂相托

你哭泣
我以怀相拥

你微笑
我以唇相敬

My heart, my eyes saw and felt something invisible, I have a strong feeling about it, that what I see and feel is what we call art. It is the deep truth of life, such as the Black Woman, just a jobless, normal woman, but I found a beauty from her, sad and happy.

I know sooner or later I will give thanks to this very tough experience, the ability to see real beauty is wonderful, I am in the dark but I am the person with a light in my heart. Yes, I feel this ability in my mind, I can stop to look at the lady, I found it, is a good art I can do.

A powerful beautiful light and your hands creating such amazing work.

All the things are different now I am climbing my Mountain under the storm, I am up now.

我的心我的眼睛看见和感觉到一些无形之物。我强烈地感受到我们的所见所闻，我们所称之为的艺术，其实就是生命的深层含义。就比如那个黑人女子，只是一个普通的家庭妇女，但我从她身上看到了生命的真，悲凉与幸福。

我知道迟早我要感谢这段艰难困苦的岁月，它给了我发现真实的能力，美不胜收。我身处黑暗，心中却燃了一盏灯。我感到了这种能力，它使我驻足观看一位女士，嗯我找到了，是我所能做的艺术。

强有力的光照亮美好，你的手创造神奇。

所有的一切都变了，我在暴风雨中攀登，山不在高有仙则名。

I am thinking how to build MGBO's body in one; I want to show you how you look in my eyes.

I am humbled by the thought...

I have never told you in fact I have an impression of your body; I was looking at you when you took the photo of me and your back, so it is not difficult to think about your image, and you walking, you are cool, I didn't tell you before. I am thinking of your back, your walk, your personality combines all of them but I have no idea of you naked, you know why?

I have never imagined you naked although you told me you sleep naked, as in my mind I have a very deep respect of our relationship to stop me thinking of the King of Queen. I love both of you and your loves. When I love I love deeply without being selfish. When I hate I hate deeply with sword shining.

I understand this very much, you are in my heart.

I think for this reason you and me can make something very good as we understand real love. I still can make the Mountain, Gardener, Bear and Ox's body.

我在琢磨如何将忙叔的多重性体现在一个人体雕塑里。我想向你展示我眼中的你什么样。

我很荣幸被你想象……

我从未提起过,事实上,我注意过你的身体。当你为我拍照时,我也在观看你。所以想象你的身体并不是件难事儿。我以前没说,你走起路来很酷。我想到你的背影,你行走时的样子,你的个性体现在其中。但我无法想象你的裸体。你知道吗,我从未想过你的裸体,尽管你告诉我你裸睡。因为我非常尊重我们之间的友谊,我很尊重家长。对你们是爱屋及乌。爱就忘我,恨则寒光如剑。

我深深地明白,你在我心深处。

因为对爱的正确理解,我想你和我会做些出色的东西。我还是可以做一个忙叔的混合体。

I always remember when you were in Manchester train station, I turned my head I saw you were behind me, your head say come on to me, very cool, I am very proud of you.

I respect you deeply; I look at you many times, creating.

Its ok for you to look at me, we are artists; it doesn't compromise our positions... You seem not happy about your belly, I don't think it is not good, that is you and you are relaxed but logical.

I feel it is ugly, it's all people see at first.

I understand, I should look at you as an artist, yes, of course.

As artists we have to let our imaginations be free to go wherever they want. Nothing can stop a real artist. Today we have created much with our words, yes, it comes by nature and it is the feeling. Yes, it is.

我一直记得那次你在曼城皮卡迪里火车站，我转过头看见你正站在我身后，你用了甩脑袋示意我过去，很酷，我很得意。

我非常尊重你，你的创作，我也在关注你。

看我没事儿，艺术家吗！那并不影响什么。

你似乎很不满意你的肚子，我到不觉得有什么，那就是你吗。你很松弛，但赋有逻辑。

我觉得丑，人们第一眼看见你的就是肚子。

我明白，我应该把你当艺术家看待，当然。

作为艺术家，我们应该天马行空，无拘无束。真正的艺术家是没有阻碍的。今天我们用文字进行大量地创作。那是对大自然的感受与直觉。

Thank you for the pictures, Japanese opera is a very concentrated culture of the Nation; from it we can feel the authentic style of the Country. I am happy you got some ideas from Kabuki. It looks similar to Chinese local theatre. It is rooted in the ancient life, but growing up by time; it is a real art if we can appreciate it.

感谢你发来的照片。日本戏剧是日本民族文化的浓缩，从中你可以领受到这个国家的真正的风格。

很高兴知道你从日本歌舞伎中得到灵感。它们应该类似于中国的传统地方戏曲。它们植根于古老的民间生活，又不断地与时俱进。如果懂得欣赏的话，那才是真正的艺术。

This is the one, sculptured by my imagination, MGBO naked and sleeping.

Wonderful... It's me... I love it...

Do you really like it? Yes, it is you in my mind. My skill is still beginning, but it looks better than the one with high skill; I feel more feeling and emotion with every sculpture I make. However, my skill needs to improve as many feelings I can't express because of the low skill.

I have got the post card from Japan by MGBO, that's so nice, the Fuji Mountain. I like it, that Mountain reminds me that I miss my Mountain, it moved out and will move back soon.

Somehow get the Mountain on the plane on Sunday...

这就是那个，我想象的忙叔的合体裸睡雕塑。

没错，是我，我挺喜欢的。

你真喜欢吗？是的，我心目中的你。我是个初学者的水平，但看上去拙朴。每一个雕塑我都用情感和感觉去做。当然必须提高技术才能准确表达内心的真实感动。

我收到了忙叔从日本寄来的明信片，非常精致，富士山，我喜欢，它让我想起忙叔，他出门了但很快就会回来。

无论如何，忙叔周日的航班。

Skill will always improve with time but feeling and emotion is what makes you an artist...

I do understand what you said, yes, it is feeling and emotion that drives my hands to be brave and make art. I am confident of my feeling more now. And my emotion, I know what I see…

A Poem in This Morning
Zaiming Wang (May 2016)

Four red brick walls and a name
If you have never broken the door
Trying to go inside
That is all the things
You can know of a house
Our eyes were stop by stop.

熟能生巧，感知和情感才是成为艺术家的要素。

我非常理解你所说的。感觉和情感驱动我的双手勇敢地做艺术，现在我对我的直觉自信多了，至于情感我情故我在。

清早的诗
王再鸣（2016年5月）

四面红墙
一个名字
如果不破门而入

这就是
你对一所房子
所知的全部

我们的双目
由于阻碍
而被停止

I am thinking of making another body sculpture to show you, then I got this good news; Mountain, Gardener, Bear and Ox are back.

Welcome MGBO Peter back home. It is so nice you are in your own bed now, you should be tired. I am happy you come back. I give you a big kiss, big hugs and big smile, from Yellow Flower, Milk Lady and Firework.

Love your smile... Mountain back home and the Gardener ready to start watering duty again. The Bear will have more dreams about Yellow Flower and Firework and the Ox is waiting for Milk Lady...

我本打算再做一个人体雕塑给你看看。然而,我得到一个好消息,忙叔,园叔,奥先生,奥克思回来啦。

欢迎回来,真是温馨,你躺在自己的床上了。你应该很累吧。我很快乐你回来啦,给你一个重吻,一个深拥和一个咧嘴笑。来自黄玫,挤奶媛和小钢炮。

喜欢看到你笑,忙叔回来后,园叔要打理花园,奥先生会做更多美梦,关于小黄和小钢炮。奥克思在等挤奶媛。

Yellow Flower Blooming
Zaiming Wang (May 2016)

I saw the Yellow Flower grow
To be a big tree in the sunset glow
The sky was warm colourful
Nature is so great teaching us about beauty
I hope you have a good sleep last night
Bear need have a rest then refresh
Gardener needs to work again.

I really love Yellow Flower Blooming. It's great to see your work gaining strength... Do you think making bodies has given you a new perception?

Thank you very much for your good words for my artwork, that is most important to encourage me to keep working hard on it. I do like to make sculptures, faces and bodies now. Yes, making body has given me more ideas and freedom to express the feelings of my heart. It has made my blood flow stronger. I am learning from process of making.

黄花开
王再鸣（2016年5月）

日落时
黄花开 成
一棵树

天空涂满红霞
现出她的
美丽模样

愿你安睡
愿你早起
愿你把我打理

我很喜欢黄花开，见到你的工作有了成效很欣慰。你觉得做人体雕塑会给你新的灵感吗？

非常荣幸你对我的作品的夸奖，对我来说这是莫大的鼓舞。我很喜欢做这些头像和身体的小雕塑。是的，做人体给了我更多的灵感，也是我更自由地表达情感，常常是热血沸腾，创作过程正是学习的过程。

I Fell Asleep
Peter Lay (May 2016)

I fell asleep
Awake now,
The Bear is feeling stiff
As the light comes
Creeping across the sky
Bringing a new day
To my jet-lagged mind.

The Mountain is softly snoring
Feeling the roots of the Yellow Flower
The Gardener is close to waking
Then watering
Both Firework and Flower.

Meanwhile
The Ox awaits the Milk Lady
And the Sword Warrior stands guard
Whilst all around her slumber
Except the Bear
Who is awake?
Smiling and stretching.

I can see a picture of all of us there, from inside and outside, surface and mind, loving and beautiful, desiring and caring. Patient and calm, ready for the big day coming. Yes, I have many feelings of art to talk to you about, and some ideas that have changed by time and my new experience... Art should be fluid, ever ready to change, and you were away, enjoying the exotic, now taking time to get used to being back home.

入眠
彼得-雷（2016年5月）

我睡了
又醒

奥先生细听自己的喘息
光缓缓地
从天空铺下来

点亮了
新的一天

我在哪
日本还是
英格兰

忙叔轻鼾
蔷薇低吟
爆竹起舞
园叔梦醒

姑娘牧牛
壮士佩剑

谁醒了
微笑着抻着腰

画里画外，心里眼里，美和爱，欲望和关怀，全部交织在一起。平静和耐心地等待新的一天降临。是的，我有许多感受希望与你分享，但随着时间经历的变化，想法也时过境迁。艺术是流动的，一直在变化着。你离开去享受异域风情了。回来还的适应一阵儿。

MGBO, this is why you got the name, means I do understand how you are, and who you are. And I am confident about our art work. My private life has become part of this art now, it is very hard to deal with alone, but I get the energy from this against being hurt deeply. I turned my mind and my passion to create with the bad experience instead of just crying, even crying is powerful now. I have learnt a lot of things through it; I am expecting to share all of them with you. I am looking forward to seeing you.

MGBO
Peter Lay (May 2016)

So here is MGBO
Laying naked beneath the sheets
Awake since 4.30am.
Dozing, dreaming, thinking,
Wondering, musing, considering.
Feeling a little de-connected,
With everything and everyone.

MGBO is forever, you always feel you owe your love to all, I use my heart to be your friend, and so I will be the best one.

忙园奥奥克思，这是为什么你得了这个名字，它意味着我对你的了解。

我对我们所做的事情充满信心。现在我的个人生活也成了我们工作的一部分。我一个人还真无以应对，你的加入给了我抵御被深度伤害的能量。百炼钢化绕指柔。眼泪也是子弹飞。我期待着与你见面并分享这些经历。

MGBO
彼得-雷（2016年5月）

瞧　那哥几个
拂晓时
红毯裹身
打盹　游曳　思寻
好奇　冥想　打算

如痴如醉如梦如幻

永远的你们啊，你总觉得你欠他们一份爱，我用心做你的朋友，用此，我就成了你最好的知交。

I am thinking about pictures on the beach totally wet body in the very thin dress, the water dripping.

And I am thinking of the red Chinese dress, tight made with elastic fabrics, moulding it to the body, for dancing. I will have one made if I get a chance to go back to China, or I will make it myself one day.

I am thinking I should learn to sew these costumes for taking pictures in the long term, such as short yellow dress, tight red cheongsam dress and the very thin dress for the water of the beach.

So, are you emerging from the water in a thin yellow dress?

I am thinking totally wet, whole body, with dress sticking to body and water dripping from the dress, hair and body. Standing in front of the water line or with some background, or half in the water...

The wet dripping pictures I call it 'Weeping', the whole body is crying from deep heart, because of a lot of sadness in this world.

I think I am changing, I can feel myself.

When my friends are talking, I just listen like a bystander, but my initial reaction is to join them, I feel I am looking at life. I can very easily cry now, as I can see the sad part of people even though they don't show you.

I must think about the sad part as a real part of life, as well as the beautiful part...

我在考虑海边的照片，全身湿透，薄连衣裙往下滴水。

还有红色的紧身旗袍，弹性塑形面料，穿着跳舞。如果有机会回去我再去做一条，或者自己做。

从长计议，我也在考虑自己学做服装，黄色的短装连衣裙，红色紧身旗袍，还有适合海边用的薄裙子。

你会像清水出芙蓉那样从水里露出来吗？

我是想全身湿透，裙子贴在身上，水滴从头发和身体往下滴。站在海岸线上或者有些背景或者一半没在水中。

这个滴水的照片我叫它"哭泣"，因为这世间有太多的伤心事，整个身体从心向外哭泣。

我可以感觉到自己在改变。

当朋友聊天时我好像一个旁观者聆听，我即观看生活又参与其中。轻易就哭了，好像总能看到人们内心的悲伤。

我认为悲伤是生活的真实，就如美丽一样。

We talked about sad yesterday, I have found sad is a very beautiful feeling to see, because people show the very true side of life.

I think I understand what you are saying, beautiful to see, but beautiful to feel?

Yes, I think feeling is very important for art, sad always touches our feeling.

I tend to look on the bright side of life, am generally happy, so it's difficult for me look at things that way, I find it hard to see your sadness, I will try harder to look beyond my initial senses, to try and find this beauty you talk about...

I understand you and I can see you are the happy MGBO. Happy is powerful to deal with tough life. In pictures, can you tell the stories behind the beautiful smiling faces?

昨天我们讨论了悲伤，我发现悲伤很美，因为人们悲伤时很真实。

我想我明白你的意思，看上去美，感觉呢，也美吗？

嗯，感觉很重要，悲伤打动心灵。

我注重生活光明的一面，总的来说，我比较乐观，很难以你的角度去看生活的悲哀。我将尝试超越我的直觉去看你所说的这种美。

我明白也看得出来你的生活是快乐的，乐观是战胜艰难生活的力量。从照片中你能看出来美丽笑容背后的故事吗？

I may have time to make sculpture at home in the morning, I will see... A kiss for you... Oh, Queen still sleeping, so step lightly.

Thank you very much MGBO, now the Gardener has come back, the Yellow Flower will bloom again. I am thinking of starting to write my biography now.

The Gardener is happy to be back and looking forward to seeing the Yellow Flower blooming again...

She will bloom again and stronger than before, the root in deeper underneath the Mountain.

Wonderful.

What I want to say is what we see of the life is just a surface phenomenon, it is not the truth. I want to express two ideas of my view of life; first is that life is not the reality we see, second the life should be the one of our dreams, this is why we have dreams and the artist's job exists.

我今早可能有时间在家做小雕塑，再看吧。给一个飞吻。啊，家长还睡觉呢，那脚步轻点儿。

非常感激你。园叔回来了，花园又要春意盎然了。我想开始写关于自己的故事。

园叔也很高兴回来了，期待着满园春色。

它们会开得更加茂盛，因为它们已深深扎根于斯。

妙哉！

我想说的是，我们眼睛所看到的生活只是一种现象，不是本质。我想表达我对生活的两个观点。首先，生活并非如我们日常所见；再者，生活应该是原梦。这就是梦与艺术存在的原因。

Good morning MGBO, it is good to know all of you have a good sleep and dreams. Yes, I have a good sleep but always wake up in middle of night, so I sleep during the day, as the Yellow Flower needs to bloom after the watering.

Bear sounds very nice and happy now; I miss all Mountain, Gardener, Bear and Ox.

We miss you too Yellow Flower, and always happy to hear about your new thinking. The Bear had a good sleep and is now having a big stretch...

Glad to know you have a good sleep last night; hope you had a sweet dream as well.

Bear always wakes with a smile on his face...

早上好,很高兴知道你们睡得梦得都好。是啊,我也睡得不错,就是半夜总会醒来。所以我白天睡觉,就如喝足了水后开放的花朵。

听起来奥先生美滋滋的,我想念大家。

我们也想念你们。听你谈自己的想法总是很开心。奥先生睡醒了满意地伸展着四肢。

很欣慰知道你睡得不错,希望你还梦得不错。

奥先生总是喜笑颜开地醒来。

I was woken up by my thoughts and tried to sleep longer, I am thinking of the fresh morning. I am thinking that a bird doesn't need advice about the dangers of flying. Do you see freedom from flying, freedom to be oneself, to be able to fly and soar through the sky? If we are birds we can fly, we feel we can understand what real freedom is, more than the people who said they love freedom but are afraid of flying.

We are all chained to the earth in some way, fighting our battles, many at the cost of others. Is this our dialogue of freedom in the book?

Yes, this is what I am thinking recently, who are we, how and why are we living in this or that way?

As an individual, we are father or mother, son or daughter, teacher or student, friend or partner, in society, but in the evening in the bed, when we are ourselves, when we talk to our soul mate, we have different feelings.

Yes, it is a very big question, I just try to find the small part of it, how to make the honest sculptures. In fact the answer is from the different people's lives, their faces and their bodies.

So, in life we have responsibilities and we try to find time within this to be ourselves, to explore our feelings and passions.

As artists we express this, we are honest to ourselves, we create, we love, we fly.

Yes, I think so; art is the way to express our honest feeling of life.

我被我的思想吵醒了，本想多睡一会，又想到有一个清……
我想鸟无需被告知飞翔的危险，你看见飞翔的自由吗？在空中翱翔成为自由的自己的能力。我们比那些热爱自由却惧怕飞翔的人更懂得自由的意味。

我们都以不同的方式被束缚，我们努力成为自己，也为他人付出代价。这就是书本中关于自由的对话吗？

是啊，我最近也在想这个事，我们是谁我们将以怎样的方式生存，为什么？

作为个体，我们在社会中是父亲或母亲，儿子或女儿，教师或学生，朋友或搭档。但是，每当夜深人静，独自一人时，我们与自己的灵魂交谈，感觉是不一样的。

这是个很大的话题，我只是试图发现冰山一角，有助于我的小雕塑。事实上，答案就在每个人的生活中，他们的脸上和身体里。

我对生活负有责任，同时我们努力成为自己，发现自己的情感和感受。

艺术家表达自己，忠实于自己的感受，创作，爱，飞翔。

我同意，艺术是对生活真实的再现。

Creating in art is freedom as we needn't worry if somebody doesn't understand; the art is in the creation, we just express our own view.

Yes, our view, not everyone will agree or see it.

Creating is same as the flying, not always the same, but sometimes according to the experience of life people have a different understanding. Chicken can't understand Eagle's happiness, and Chicken may think Eagle is fool. But Eagle doesn't laugh at Chicken and doesn't feel sorry for Chicken, we all were born predestined.

As artists we use everything in our creations, our experiences, things we have seen, have felt, people we know, have known, our philosophy, our love, our passion, in fact we put everything into it, our whole beings...

That's a big truth, now I see, sensitive feeling and soul, but true to ourselves.

艺术创作是自由的，你无需顾及别人懂不懂你，你只是在表达自己。

对，自己的观点，不求人人都理解。

创作就如飞翔，每一次都不同，人们对艺术的理解取决于人们生活的经历。就如鸡无法明白鹰的快乐，也许还认为鹰笨笨。但鹰既不嘲笑鸡也不怜悯它，一切皆为前世注定。

艺术家以生活为创作蓝本，人生经历，感受，曾经相识的人，现在相处的人，生活的方式，爱，激情，一切的一切。

大实话，你看，灵感，灵魂，最重要的是忠实于自己。

Every artist develops their own artistic process.

Yes, I have read a lot of artist's creative background; everyone has a different life experience, different mind and feeling of the world. So I just think the critic doesn't even know what they are talking about, they sometimes destroy the meaning of the works.

There are lots of ways to bring art to life, the artist or artists must find the right path for them to do so. You and I are developing a process, whether we are working together or separately, we are entwined, through communicating, feeling... The process runs through everything we do, it is our art, our passion, our life. It is in your sculptures, in my pictures, in the scenarios we create, it is growing and very much in our writing.

每位艺术家都以其不同的方式创作。

嗯，我读过很多艺术家创作的事迹，他们有着不同的生活经历，不同的头脑，和对世界的不同感受。从这个意义上说，批评家有时是不知所云。他们有时会曲解作品的真意。

有许多方法将艺术融入生活。艺术家必须找到正确的途径去创作。你和我就在这个过程中。无论我们合作工作，还是各自独立创作，我们始终保持沟通并贯穿始终。不论你的雕塑，我的摄影，以及我们设定的艺术情境，它在不断完善并运用于我们的写作。

It is good, I think, that we come from different cultural backgrounds, we have different everyday life, but we communicate to share and to combine ideas. That is more powerful than two people live in the same circumstances and have the same ideas.

That may be so.

I feel it so, it is a wonderful morning the Gardener and Mountain do a lot of work, the Yellow Flower is ready to bloom again.

The Yellow Flower inspires them, her blooms are so beautiful.

真好。我们来自不同的文化背景，日常生活也各不相同，但是我们相互交流，乐于分享，彼此认同。这远比来自同一生长环境，有着同样想法的人们之间的交流要更有利。

也许吧。

我是这么认为的。一个晴朗的早上，忙叔和园叔已经忙了半天了。花儿又要开了。

小黄激励着他们。她的绽放是那么的动人。

I wanted to make more Figures but I found that the more I desire to make more sculptures the less I have feeling about it. I am thinking the Sword Warrior, the standing body...

Just let your hands and fingers do the work...

Two things I need to find out how to make better hands, instead of sword in left hand, I make two hands in the Buddha shape that we call 'water lily flower finger', it means peace. Another problem I have is how to make it stand as the material is too soft to stand. The flower is more powerful than the sword this is my idea of the sculpture Sword Warrior.

我渴望多做一些人物雕塑。但我发现，越是刻意期待越没感觉，欲速则不达。我想的是佩剑女侠和站立的人体。

那就把这个工作交付给你的手和手指吧。

有两件事我必须弄明白，与其左手握剑，我做成两只佛手的手型。我们称之为莲花指。象征和平，另一个问题，如何使人体雕塑站立？因为材料太软。

花比剑更有力量。这是我关于剑侠要表达的意境。

Hello Yellow Flower, Little Firework, Sword Warrior and Milk Lady. Mountain, Gardener, Bear and Ox wish you a good morning...

Good morning, MGBO. Yellow Flower, Firework and Milk Lady wish you have a good day today and we are wondering did you have a sweet dream last night.

I don't often remember my dreams but I often wake thinking of you and our work.

That's true, we don't often remember the dream even the ones just before we wake up, Bear is so nice to be thinking of me when he open his eyes, thanks, I am thinking of you too...

Bear is smiling.

喂，小黄小钢炮剑侠还有挤奶媛，忙叔园叔奥先生和奥克思问你们早上好。

早上好各位，小组成员祝你们有美满的一天。这边厢好奇地打听一下昨晚做梦了没有？

我通常不太记得我的梦，但我醒来的时候会想起你以及我们的工作。

是这样的，我们通常不记得我们梦到了什么，甚至于醒来之前的最后那个梦。奥先生真好，睁开眼睛就想起我，多谢你，我也想着你。

奥先生笑了。

I have seen the web page you created, very nice, thank you very much MGBO. The picture is great, I love that picture, I am so proud of your work. You are a very good photographer I think from the pictures you took of me, this picture makes me think about who I am, I like the lady myself. I look calm of spirit and full of dreams. That is exactly me.

Glad you like it, you may have seen it before, I just cropped it...

Yes, I like it very much, thank you. I don't remember seeing that picture but I like it very much, very natural, very me.

我看了你设计的网页，很好。谢谢你，照片挺不错，喜欢，为你自豪。从你为我拍的照片看，我认为你是个好摄影师。这张照片让我想到我是谁这个问题。我喜欢照片中这位女士，看上去很平静，充满梦想，那正是我。

你喜欢让我很欣慰。你以前可能见到过，我只是裁剪了一下。

是啊，我很喜欢，非常感谢。我不记得之前看到过，不过非常自然，非常像我。

June 2016

2016年6月

Can you explain for me the meaning of domesticate?

Domesticate:

Tame an animal and keep it as a pet or on a farm for food.

Also to cultivate a plant for food, for example, rice, potatoes, wheat.

Or make someone fond of and good at home life, like a housewife.

It is what I want to express, that human beings are domesticated by so called civilization. Knowledge keeps them far from their nature, so they lose their instinctive understanding from their own senses. People respect and are proud of how much knowledge they have, ignoring our senses. What I am interested in is feeling the nature part of human beings. I have found a lot of difference inside the way of the 'Chinese faces'. It is not flower it is grass, are animals content to be domesticated and eaten, or the cow to be milked twice a day…

Women have long been domesticated… What do you mean, difference inside the way of the 'Chinese faces'?

可以解释一下"驯化"这个词吗？

驯化：

驯养一种动物使之成为宠物，或者作为农场的食物。

也有种植植物作为食物，比如稻谷，土豆，小麦。

再有使某人乐于和善于家务，比如家庭主妇。

这正是我想要表达的。人类正在被所谓的"文明"驯化。知识使人类远离自然，从而失去了依赖本能和直觉去理解自然的能力。人们崇尚和得意于他们获得知识的多少，而忽略直觉。我感兴趣的是人类自身自然的那部分。我看到大量的"中国面孔"内在的方面。那不是花，是草。动物接受被驯化和成为食物，亦或奶牛一天要挤两次奶。

妇女长期被驯化，你说什么呢？中国面孔的内在不同方面？

I have had contact with many Chinese women recently, I am reading their faces trying to read their inside while talking, and I found they are domesticated by the mainstream education though, very deeply. The heart closed tightly and the way to think is same.

It's a complicated subject; you could say that women are naturally domesticated for a length of time by childbirth and immediate after care, feeding etc.

No matter if they are satisfied or worrying, feel like the machine, even the pictures shown to public is the same way, eating food, famous landscapes, children and friends. How beautiful, how delicious, how good.

最近我接触了许多中国女性，当我与她们交谈时，试图读出她们的内心想法，我发现她们被主流思想影响得很深。内心紧锁，思维雷同。

这是一个复杂的话题，妇女被自然地驯化为分娩，看护，喂养的主体。

无论她们开心还是担心，已成为一种机械化行为。甚至向公众展示的照片也是这样，吃，风景，孩子和朋友。很美很香很好。

Lots of men like to tie their women to the home; some countries believe it should be that way.

I see, in China a lot women tied themselves at home to their men.

Everywhere I think.

Women thinking their life is linked to the men, otherwise they feel scared and lost.

Yes, but women are not just cleaners to look after the home or baby machines.

I think part of reason is from nature, part of reason is education.

This is true, but for a long time women have been disempowered by it, because the laws of the social game are made by men. Women have to learn more than men to understand and play it well, it does not fit women's instinct and most of us are living by instinct.

I think this is generally true and not really changing much, I believe.

I think the right comes from desire of our heart. I believe just do it, of course we have to think how to do it before do it, we have to see and understand the ways things are, this will give us a basis to move forward, if we can't agree on what is, how can we possibly agree on what might be?

很多男人喜欢女人守在家里，在有些文化里认为女人就应该在家。

哦，在中国一些女性为了男人自己情愿守在家。

哪里都一样，我想。

那些女性认为她们的命运是依附于男人的，否则，她们就感到恐惧和失落。

是这样，但女性并非只是搞卫生，照顾家，带孩子的家庭保姆。

我想部分原因处于天性，还有教育。

的确如此，久而久之女性权利被剥夺，因为社会规则由男人制定，女性要花费更多的精力去理解和适应。因为这不符合女性的本能，女人很多时候是依赖本能生活的。

总的来说是这样，并且我相信并无多少改变。

我们的权利来源于我们内心的渴望。我坚信行动力，当然也要三思而后行。我们要循自然的规律，这是我们所有行为的依据。皮之不存，毛将焉附。

I have a lot of bad experience of my own; I am frustrated all the time, but I meet the Mountain, Gardener, Bear and Ox at last.

I'm not sure we have all the answers.

It is a philosophy, what you said, let me keep and think in my mind.

I think you have a lot to say, things that are worth listening to.

Thanks, I've met a person who makes me ask questions, no matter get answer or not. Keep moving forward, I am on the journey, it is just starting, my hand is slow but my brain is fast.

I like that.

I am trying to make whole things of life, to focus, to achieve one thing.

I have to somehow get all these beautiful words and ideas into a book.

More than one book…

More than a book…

我自己有很多不幸的经历。

我总是很挫败，但我最终遇见了忙叔园叔，老奥和小奥。

我不是很确定，所有问题都有答案。

就如你所说，这是一个哲学问题，让我在脑子里想想。

我想你有很多话要说，一些值得倾听的话。

多谢。曾经有人令我产生许多问题，不在乎是否有答案。始终向前看，人在旅途，这只是开始，我的手跟不上飞快运转的大脑。

我欣赏。

我一直在集中精力做一件事。

我会设法把这些优美的文字和美好的想法变成一本书。

不止一本书。

不仅仅是一本书。

Good morning Yellow Flower, big hug.

Oh, I thought, big hugs, is used to say goodbye, now I know we also can use it say hello!

Good any time, I think.

Any time when we think about it, I think so.

早安小黄,来个熊抱。

哦,我以为熊抱只是在分别的时候。现在明白了,它也是见面打招呼的用语。

任何时候都正是时候。

任何你想到的时候。

Depression makes creative feelings rise as the nervous and sad mood makes heart very sensitive and deeply touched. Another life is violence I can feel growing in the body, like the Firework looking for explosion, whereas I can see you are calmer with nice personality and are full of feelings about art.

I think I have found a balance in my life; this enables me to be creative and to see creativity in others. I found a new role in life as a Gardener, recognised and named by you.

You are helping me make my negative life become the positive.

沮丧有助于提高创造性。因为紧张和伤感更能触动内心深处，更敏感。一个暴力的生命在身体里涌动，就如炮仗即将爆发。然而，我看见你冷静温和的个性，充满了艺术的感觉。

我找到了生命中的平衡，这使我有能力去创造，同时理解别人的创作。我找到了生命中的新角色园丁。被你这个千里马发现和命名的伯乐。

你使我们生命焕然一新。

Thank you for the morning greeting my Gardener, and all MGBO, the more things become difficult the more I feel you are here in my heart, which makes me stronger in spirit to deal with any trouble in my life. I never forget about our art, we will do great work on it I think, right?

Of course we will do great art, keep strong.

I have feelings of pressure but I get stronger in mind, of course I cried, I hated, I frustrated, but after, I become stronger. My body full of salt, so my tears and my blood, is strong taste.

Love your words.

Thank you, when I talk to you I am thinking who is listening to me, so the words jump into my mind. What I want to say is the more the pressure the more strong I have got in my mind. Chocolates give me energy as well, I have them always. When I am talking to you I follow my feeling, you always understand me by my words, I feel very happy and your understanding encourages my writing, the Important thing is that I found we have similar feelings and ideas in many things, especially in the aesthetic concept of beauty. This is the basis and the reason I have a lot of ideas when I talk to you.

Yes, I feel we have a special bond; we are becoming ever more successful at portraying and interpreting our ideas.

Yes, I agree.

园叔谢谢清晨的问候，谢谢大家。 越是艰难的时候，越是感觉你是那么的近，近在我心里。这使我有强大精神力量去抵御生活中的种种困难。我从未忘记我们的艺术。我们将会做得很有意义，对吗？

那当然，我们要做真正的艺术，要有信心。

我一直有压力，但我内心坚强，我哭，我恨，我感到挫败，但这一切让我变得更强壮。我体内充满了盐，所以我的眼泪和血充满了浓郁的铁味。

喜欢你的文字。

谢谢夸奖。因为我知道谁在倾听，所以那些话语自然地跳进我的头脑里。我想说的是，我是越挫越勇那样的人。巧克力带给我能量，我随身携带着。与你谈话是跟着感觉，你能透过文字明白我，我很欣慰，你的这种理解成为我写作的动力。重要的是我发现我们在许多事情上感觉和看法很相似。尤其是对美学意义上的美的观念。每当与你交谈就产生许多想法。

是，特殊的纽带将我们相连接。

我们越来越心照不宣地彼此描绘和诠释各自的想法。

我同意你的观点。

I have no words to tell how much I thank you in my heart with tears. I put them in my heart and mind. You have a good day with my wishes.

Big kiss.

How big?

Very big.

Strong Sunshine strong mind
Peter Lay (2016)

Strong sunshine
Strong mind
Strong woman

Beautiful woman
Beautiful mind
Beautiful sunshine

Wonderful sunshine
Wonderful woman
Wonderful mind

文字无法表达我的心含热泪的感激之情,真心诚意。并衷心祝愿你开心又一天。

一个大大的吻。

多大?

非常大!

热烈的阳光 澎拜的心
彼得-雷(2016年)

阳光热烈
心澎拜

多彩世界
温柔人

天空雪白
红唇一缕

I am missing you, I feel very sad about the things happening around me and you are the only person I want to cry in front of. I have found a yellow flower, after the bloom, it becomes the seeds flying on the air and rooted in the Mountain everywhere, a Dandelion. Bear is hungry, this flower is too small, barely a mouthful, just for taste. But I remember Bear is afraid of one type of large yellow flower, they can cause him dizziness.

That is Rapeseed.

我很想念你,近来发生的事令我很难过。你是我唯一可以哭诉的人。花开过后,我发现了小黄花,它变成一粒粒种子在空中飞舞,四处散落在山里。奥先生很饥饿,一棵蒲公英花朵太小,连一口都不够,只够舔舔味道。但我记得,奥先生对一种大黄花过敏,看了会眩晕。

那是油菜花。

I do remember what you told me, hate will eat me up inside, my heart should be full of love and beauty. With my love for the Mountain I will bloom strong and grow into a beautiful flower. I never forget about it and never give up trying my best to make the next one and the next one, better and better. I mean the sculptures.

I figured that....

The Mountain appreciates your love and loves the blooms; the Mountain, Gardener, Bear and Ox loves Yellow Flower, the Sword Warrior, the Milk Lady and the Little Firework.

我当然记得你对我的告诫，仇恨会腐蚀心灵。我们的心灵应该充满美好的爱。因为我有一个好伯乐，我要做一个千里马。我始终记得从没忘记尽全力做最好，人生，雕塑。

我理解。

伯乐为他的千里马自豪。不论她有着怎样多重的性格和个性，我对她都寄托着不同的感受和愿望。

Yellow Flower feels very happy to think of MGBO, I have slept and woke up now, I appreciate you from heart, and this is fate driving me to go in the art direction with my whole life. Good morning, is Bear still awake and stretching or fall asleep again?

Awake and feeling romantic.

Plato's romantic?

Now that's an interesting thought but I think the Bear is just feeling amorous.

Amorous is a new word I have learnt now. That means Bear is very romantic and he is hiding in the big Mountain somewhere.

He is, not always hiding though.

Sentimental or passionate?

More passionate than sentimental.

I see, but it is a nice Bear anyway, I think Bear is the soul of the Mountain, Gardener work very hard and we will see his great job by the blooms, which is the Yellow Flower's answer to the big love from the Mountain, Gardener, Bear and Ox, 'Yellow Over The Mountain.'

每想到你我就快乐起来。我刚醒了，我从心里感激你。是命运的驱使，我用生命去热爱艺术。早安，奥先生醒了吗？

醒着，想着浪漫的事。

柏拉图式的浪漫？

这个想法挺有意思。奥先生叫奥莫罗斯，因为他很多情。

多情的奥莫罗斯，我才知道这个意思呢。也就是说，奥先生浪漫，只是时常躲在山角落里。

是这样，然而也不全是。

多愁善感还是激情澎拜呢？

激情大于多愁。

嗯，总之他很善良，他是忙叔的灵魂。从满园芬芳可以看到园叔辛勤的劳动。那也是黄玫对园叔以及所有得到的爱的报答。是这爱把黄玫高高托起。

Feast of Colour
Peter Lay (2016)

Glorious dreams of dazzling yellow
A vision of beauty shimmering in light
Blooming and opening with the dawn
A sumptuous feast for the coming morn.

色彩的盛宴
彼得-雷（2016年）

炫目的明黄
挤满了梦乡

零星的波光
敲打眼眶
忽明忽暗的拂晓啊
你正为来自故乡的色彩
展开奢华的盛装

I feel happy that you like the sculpture I made this morning. I found that art should be the expression of our philosophy, every line and every curve; I am excited, thinking of this idea of art.

You have a good sleep and sweet dream, if you are already sleeping; I hope you can feel my greeting in your dream.

Thank you for coming into my dream.

我很高兴你喜欢我今早做的这个雕塑。我认为艺术应该表达我们的哲学观，通过每一条线，每一个弧度。我为这个想法激动不已。如果你已经睡了，就希望你好梦好觉，并且在梦中收到我的祝福。

谢谢你来到我的梦里。

I'm looking at another sculpture, of woman, it reminds me of some ancient goddess, I will keep practicing and getting ideas from people, not to copy, but to create my own style of sculpture, this is what I am thinking and trying to do.

Of course, keep practising and developing, keep true to your own style, that's important.

Yes, I agree that I must practice a lot to find my way with my own experience as a Yellow Flower. I am enjoying growing up in the true life with love. Thank you for the idea of practising the position and take pictures, to help create the sculptures, simple is powerful, I still believe in it. My Gardener always gives me energy and courage.

我在看另一个女人的雕塑。她使我想起一个古代的女神。我要多练习，从人群中寻找灵感。不只是复制，是创造自己风格的作品。我正在这么思考和练习呢。

没错，不断练习和提高，坚持你自己的风格，这很重要。

我也这么想，大量的练习和不断的思考才能形成自己的风格，融合了自己的体验和个性的风格。我很珍惜在充满爱的真实生活中成长。谢谢你关于反复练习以及拍照片的建议，这有助于创作。简单而有力，我始终相信这一点。伯乐一如既往地鼓励和引导我。

We see a lot of wild flowers and trees with nice small blooms, they are very attractive eyes. Suddenly I feel the small Yellow Flower was crying, under the sunshine. The dark background makes the Flower cry so the tears are blue.

I was thinking another thing our brain and body are tied and limited by the variety of thoughts and law.

What do you mean by tied and limited by variety of thoughts and law?

I meant we are told and we tell ourselves, we can't do this, we can't do that. I was trying to make a sculpture of that (Matisse) paper cut this evening when I came back, but it is not easy.

It's a flat, two dimensional image, with no structure, a three dimensional figure needs a structure, so it's difficult, and you will need to find a way to interpret it.

I just like this figure, empty is a good idea to make it simple and abstract.

Empty?

The empty parts of the cut paper; I remember Henry Moore's sculptures.

Oh yes, I remember.

我们看见许多开满鲜花的树和野花，它们是那样的耀眼。突然我感到小黄在阳光下哭泣，深色背景映衬下，眼泪是蓝色的。

我想到我们的大脑和身体总是束缚于各种规章制度。

什么意思，被各种规章制度束缚？

意思是说，我们被告知，也自我告诫，我们不能这样不能那样。今晚回家后，我尝试做马蒂斯剪纸的雕塑，很困难。

那是平面二维的不需要构造。雕塑是三维的需要构造，所以困难些，你需要找到转换的方法。

我喜欢那个造型，空是一个好主意，抽象简单。

空？

剪纸中空的那部分，我记得亨利·摩尔的雕塑。

对，我也记得。

Good morning Yellow Flower, the Mountain is stirring and the Gardener is awake this morning, the Bear is still snoring and the Ox has wondered off somewhere looking for the Milk Lady.

Good morning MGBO, sounds you have a good sleep last night, are you still awake or fell asleep again.

I'm up making tea.

I have an idea of yellow blood this morning, but maybe I will try to improve my painting skill to express my feeling.

Keep going.

One view of the Mountain.

You've given form to the Mountain, wonderful.

And I painted my feeling of this moment.

I like your expression of feeling.

早上好小黄。忙叔很激动，园叔也醒了，奥先生还在打呼噜，而奥克思不知去哪儿找挤奶媛去了。

早安诸位，看起来昨晚睡得不错，你已经彻底醒了还是又去睡回笼觉了？

我已经起床给家长准备早餐了。

我有一个关于黄色血脉的想法，但我需要提高技能去表达我的感受。

别放弃。

关于忙叔的一个想象。

给忙叔一个规划，很棒啊。

我画对山的感受。

我欣赏你的表达。

I was excited to think of painting and sculptures, two dimensional and three dimensional ways to express; it will take the whole life to try.

It takes but a moment to try, then the whole of your life to pursue.

Yes, this is my feeling of the art life. I want to create my own way, sometimes I refuse to follow other people's idea, in fact to study is to learn from other people's idea, not imitating. Open mind and open eyes is necessary and important to create, as we are living in the world which link each other.

I think occasionally we come across people in our lives that we really connect with, we like, we admire.

想到绘画与雕塑，我兴奋不已。用二维和三维不同的方法去表达自己，用一生去探索。

你需要一段时间去尝试，然后用整个一生去追求。

是啊，这是我对艺术的理解。我想形成自己的风格。有时我拒绝跟从他人的想法。事实上，所谓学习是了解别人的思路，而不是模仿。对于创作来说开放的头脑和敏锐的眼光是重要的也是必要的。我们居住在一个彼此关联的世界里。

生活中我们偶尔遇到那些与我们息息相关的人，那些使我们有好感和令我们钦佩的人。

I will try to make things well, I always do. This is life, life is always trying to do our best in what we are doing, and life is art in different way.

What is Life?
Peter Lay (2016)

What is life?
Life is a performance
Performance is art
Art is life.

I love it...

我总是试图把事情做好。这是生活，生活总要全力以赴。生活是艺术的另一形式。

生活是什么？
彼得-雷（2016年）

什么是生活
一场演出
演出一场
技艺人生

我喜欢！

Once I woke up I am thinking good morning to my Gardener and Mountain, Bear and Ox as well.

Good morning Yellow Flower, your Mountain and Gardener are awake, Bear is still dreaming, and the Ox has gone for a walk.

That's good they are doing their thing, Bear having long sleep, and must be good dream.

I think so...

Then I should to say hello to whom?

Mountain awake, Gardener getting up to make tea, oh Bear is waking now, I don't know where the Ox is, he is always wandering about, mostly on the Mountain but sometimes elsewhere. But they are all in the mind of Yellow Flower no matter where they are.

And she in theirs.

The Mountain is where the Yellow Flower is rooted, so is her cornerstone. In her mind the Gardener has a smiley face with a lot of life experience, he will be unhappy sometimes but his dreams make him smile always. Me too.

我一醒来就想着给诸位道早安。

早上好小黄，你的忙叔和园叔都醒了，奥先生还在睡梦中，奥克思出去散步了。

挺好各司其职。奥先生一定是还在做梦呢。

是啊。

那我应该跟谁打招呼呢？

忙叔醒了，园叔起身弄早餐。哦老奥刚醒，不知道奥克思去哪儿了，他总是四处游荡，大概进山了，有时他也会去其他地方。不论他们在哪儿，都在小黄的心里。

她也在他们心里。

小黄花深深扎根于大山，忙叔是她的主心骨。园叔和蔼可亲，阅历丰富。他也有烦恼，但梦想始终让他笑对人生。

There was me imagining you in the bath yesterday, and you were on the bus.

Yes, it is a fact you couldn't see where I was.

New buses with baths, maybe?

It is true, I found they changed the new bus, now with plugs in the side of seat, but there are no baths still, maybe in future.

我昨天以为你在沐浴,实际上你在公交车上。

是啊,因为你看不见我在哪儿。

也许新型公交车上有沐浴设备?

对,他们是换了新公交车,在车坐位旁边设置了充电插座。但是,还没安装沐浴设备,可能下一步会安装吧。

It doesn't feel like summer, where has the warmth gone, where is the sun?

The sun is hiding inside the Yellow Flower, maybe as the Yellow Flower blooms, the sun will reveal itself.

All the blooms respect and love the sun.

并没觉得这是夏天啊!热情去哪儿了,太阳哪儿去了?

太阳躲在小黄花里啦,也许小黄花一开放,太阳就露出来了。

所有的花开都是对太阳公公的挚爱与敬重。

I'm a little unsettled by our phone conversation yesterday, I am unsure of how we continue our work.

Sorry to confuse you yesterday. I think we need to have a good talk about our work as other people do not understand many times. Don't be sad, it is life, hard time make life become strength and make art more sharp. I need a time to resolve some problems. I need you to understand me now and not be sad.

OK...

Thank you very much...

21st June 2016

昨天的通话让我有些不知所措，我现在无法确定我们的工作将如何继续。

对不起昨天带给你的困惑。我想我们需要好好谈谈。很多时候旁人并不明白。别难过，这就是生活。苦难使生活充满张力，使艺术更敏锐。给我一点时间去解决一些问题。我目前非常需要你的理解，并请你开心。

好吧。

2016年6月21日

Winter's Caress
Peter Lay (January 2017)

The Mountain is dark and cold
and the Gardener is hibernating.
The Bear is wandering far and wide
and the Ox is eating the flowers.

The Yellow Flower is naked
Except for her yellow dress
Touched by the cold
Of winter's caress.

冬的爱抚
彼得-雷（2016年1月）

山幽寒
叔安寝
老奥四方野游
小奥寻花觅食

小黄
花啊

衣着单薄
只剩小小的身体

冬　依着寒冷
将她爱抚

Black Butterfly
Zaiming Wang (March 2017)

So-called civilization
is animal wearing clothes
Human beings invent lies

Hope you will
one day
agree with me

Thanks for your patience
For everything
Even for living

Black butterfly in the sky
the Grey Bear just hold her
With the top of nose.

黑蝴蝶
王再鸣 （2017年3月）

啊 文明
你为他们披上了新衣
披上新衣
他们发明了谎言

我渴望着
那一天
你和我
站着一起

我对你
充满感激
忍耐一切
耐心地活

黑蝴蝶
被高高地
举在空中

灰熊伸出
它的鼻尖

www.ingramcontent.com/pod-product-compliance
Lightning Source LLC
Chambersburg PA
CBHW070132080526
44586CB00015B/1656